We're Losing Our Minds

Rethinking American Higher Education

Richard P. Keeling and Richard H. Hersh

palgrave
macmillan

First published in 2011 by PALGRAVE MACMILLAN® in the United States—
a division of St. Martin's Press LLC, 175 Fifth Avenue, New York, NY 10010.

Where this book is distributed in the UK, Europe, and the rest of the world, this
is by Palgrave Macmillan, a division of Macmillan Publishers Limited, registered
in England, company number 785998, of Houndmills, Basingstoke, Hampshire
RG21 6XS.

Palgrave Macmillan is the global academic imprint of the above companies and
has companies and representatives throughout the world.

Palgrave® and Macmillan® are registered trademarks in the United States, the
United Kingdom, Europe and other countries.

ISBN: 978-0-230-33983-5 (paperback)
ISBN: 978-0-230-33982-8 (hardcover)

Library of Congress Cataloging-in-Publication Data

Keeling, Richard P.
   We're losing our minds : rethinking American higher education / Richard
Keeling, Richard H. Hersh.
      p. cm.
   ISBN 978-0-230-33982-8 (hardback) — ISBN 978-0-230-33983-5 1. Education,
Higher—United States. 2. Educational change—United States. 3. Education and
state—United States. I. Hersh, Richard H., 1942- II. Title.
   LA227.4.K435 2011
   378.73—dc23   2011023722

A catalogue record of the book is available from the British Library.

Design by Scribe Inc.

First edition: December 2011

D 10 9 8 7 6 5 4 3

Printed in the United States of America.

Keeling, R. P., & Hersh, R. H. (2011). *We're losing our minds: Rethinking American
higher education.* New York, NY: Palgrave Macmillan.

Contents

Preface

The purpose of this book is to get us, as a nation, talking seriously about quality in higher education. By quality we do not mean increasing access, although that is extremely important. Nor do we mean raising the rates of completion of college, although that is appropriately a high national priority as well. And we do not mean increasing the efficiency of colleges and universities or better managing the costs of higher education—undeniably also vital steps to take.

The concern that inspired this book is something more fundamental: the quantity and quality of student learning in college. Learning is what matters in higher education; questions of cost, efficiency, completion, and access, important as they are, are relevant only if students learn. We want to shift the national conversation from a primary focus on the metrics that make up magazine rankings to a serious discussion about the effectiveness of our colleges and universities in doing what they are there for: higher learning. We will make the case that there are critical gaps between what institutions of higher education promise and what they deliver.

We do this as friendly critics. Both authors have deep roots and long experience in higher education; we believe deeply—even passionately—in the ability of higher learning not only to discover, create, diversify, and apply knowledge, but also to change lives, enrich and sustain the arts and elevate culture, promote social justice, and ennoble societies and nations. We appreciate and have witnessed personally the exhausting stresses and daunting challenges that colleges and universities face today. Having served as faculty members, administrators, and leaders on campuses, and as consultants who have worked with hundreds of institutions, we know whereof we speak; we make our observations and claims carefully and conscientiously.

What we have to say is this: there is not enough higher learning in higher education. This is a critical problem that demands our urgent attention. The need for systemic institutional change—not just by one college, and not just in a few exemplary academic programs—is pressing. Nothing short of a national discussion, involving not only leaders, faculty, and students from colleges and universities, but also elected officials, education and workforce policy makers, employers, parents, and the media will generate enough energy and influence to restore learning as the first and highest priority in our colleges and universities.

There are reasons for concern about learning in the graduate and professional schools of our universities as well, but our focus in this book is on undergraduate education—college. What happens, or does not happen, in student learning in college sets the foundation for an educated population; a workforce prepared for the future's demands; a creative, engaged, and sustainable society; and a secure and peaceful nation.

"We're losing our minds" is an extraordinary judgment to make, and "rethinking higher education" rightly suggests that there is no easy or superficial solution. The title—and this book—are intended to be a call to action. Some readers will already have thought, "But what can we do? How can we change higher education?"

We write this book because there are solutions, and the solutions—while fundamental and certainly not trivial—are within our reach. Conceptual and cultural shifts are key: the establishment of a serious culture of teaching and learning, making learning the touchstone for institutional decision making and for the allocation of resources, rethinking the kind of teaching that produces learning, tightly coupling learning experiences inside and outside the classroom, defining and achieving desired learning goals, implementing regular and routine assessments of learning linked to improvement strategies, higher expectations and standards for teaching and learning, revised faculty reward systems that emphasize learning, and measuring institutional performance with metrics that really matter—indicators of true higher learning.

Can those things happen? Absolutely. Will they happen? That's up to us. Let's start talking.

Acknowledgments

Writing any book, for any author, is a lot of work. We would not claim that our challenges, as authors who are also frequently traveling consultants working together in a small higher education consulting firm, are more, or worse, than those facing other authors. But we would say that consulting with many institutions is a great privilege, and we thank our clients for their confidence and for the many conversations that have informed our reflections and contributed to our thinking.

We are fortunate that everyone in our company, Keeling & Associates, LLC (K&A), embraces, affirms, and supports our writing. It would have been much harder, and would have taken a lot longer, to write this book without the enthusiasm and assistance of our colleagues. We are especially grateful for the help given us by two members of the K&A staff: Jennifer Stevens Dickson, DrPH, director of research, and Trey Avery, a consulting associate who is now in graduate school at Teachers College, Columbia University. Their repeated and patient reading of successive drafts, many suggestions for improving the text, and diligence in checking facts and references were truly indispensable.

We thank Eric L. Engstrom, MPH, president, and Kyle J. Hutchison, senior vice president and chief of staff of K&A, for both their unflagging encouragement and the accommodations they, and their staff members, willingly made to ensure that this book made it to press.

No author writes alone; each of us depended on our partners, Eric Engstrom and Judith Meyers, for critiques, confidence, and reassurance. We offer a special acknowledgment of the nonverbal but indubitable support of Cooper D. Airedale, K&A's vice president for canine relations, whose wagging tail always told us when we were on the right track.

1

Higher Education without Higher Learning

We're Losing Our Minds

What will hold America back in this century is the quality and quantity of student learning in college. Our colleges and universities are failing to deliver true higher learning—learning that prepares graduates to meet and excel at the challenges of life, work, and citizenship. The truth is painful but must be heard: we're not developing the full human and intellectual capacity of today's college students because they're not learning enough and because the learning that does occur is haphazard and of poor quality. Too many of our college graduates are not prepared to think critically and creatively, speak and write cogently and clearly, solve problems, comprehend complex issues, accept responsibility and accountability, take the perspective of others, or meet the expectations of employers. Metaphorically speaking, we are losing our minds. This is an unacceptable and costly failure that must be resolved if we are to avoid weakening our nation's political, social, economic, scientific, and technical leadership. It is a true educational emergency.

Why has higher education abandoned higher learning? Because learning itself is no longer the first priority in most colleges and universities, despite the fact that the core mission of every institution of higher education is exactly that—learning. The many recent critiques that assail colleges and universities for rising costs, rampant inefficiencies, and insufficient accountability hit other targets but miss this key point. Without higher learning, higher education is just a series of steps that lead to a degree—the receipt of which is evidence of nothing except the completion those steps.

Bachelor's degrees have become mostly a necessary and expensive item to check off among other requirements for a job. Few undergraduate degrees really promise anything or establish legitimate expectations about the graduates who hold them. Having a bachelor's degree no longer certifies that the graduate has any specific qualifications, is capable of achieving any real intellectual depth, possesses basic workplace skills, or demonstrates personal maturity.

A painful but telling anecdote illustrates these points. A neighbor of one of the authors is the president of an international insurance consulting and actuarial firm. He frequently interviews job candidates who are recent graduates of universities in the United States and abroad. Over the course of three decades of experience, he has found U.S. graduates to be increasingly and surprisingly unprepared—not just for positions that require focus, strong cognitive skills, and a well-developed sense of personal and professional accountability, but even for the interviews themselves. "I stopped expecting them to do even basic calculations," he says, "but now most of the candidates I interview cannot think their way through a problem or tell me how they would go about solving it. How can I entrust my clients to them?" His assessment of the causes of the decline he has observed is this: "It seems that no one expected much of them in university. It's not just that they weren't challenged. No one looked to see if they were learning anything. So they have a degree, but what does that tell me?" Talk with other employers, and you will hear similar stories: American college graduates aren't adequately prepared for work.

But aren't these skills—critical thinking, problem solving, and demonstrating a sense of accountability—good examples of exactly what we should expect students to learn in college? Shouldn't we be able to assume that a college graduate can "think their way through a problem," as the actuary said? Shouldn't universities check to see what students are learning? And shouldn't they be revising and improving their educational programs if students' learning is falling short?

What level of tuition and fees would we agree to pay for a college education that does not reliably prepare students to think, work, and contribute to society? How much is that worth? We should be arguing about value, not cost alone. The problem is that without higher learning, higher education is not valuable enough to justify its price, unless you're just buying the degree, in which case a logical and savvy consumer would and should purchase the cheapest one available. The only thing that's "higher" about that kind of learning is the cost, and the combination of high cost and poor quality always equals low value.

The minds of human beings are our most precious asset. But higher education today is failing to develop, prepare, and inspire those minds and endangering our place and standing in the world. Just imagine the unrealized potential. What ideas, creations, inventions, contributions to the arts, and steps toward greater social justice are scuttled because higher learning did not happen? And in what possible alternate universe would we not take the scope and gravity of this problem seriously, and respond as quickly and forcefully as we could? Faced with any other major threat to our intellectual, economic, social, and political strength and viability, we would react at once, taking immediate measures to slow the rate of loss while we determined how to stop further losses from occurring. Confronted with a big problem, we would design big solutions. We invest a lot of money and put a lot of trust in higher education. Would we be comfortable just watching while the returns on any other investment of similar proportions dwindled?

There are solutions, and the solutions—while fundamental and nontrivial—are within our reach. Higher education must make learning the first priority; we should expect nothing less. At the heart of the matter is the need to change institutional culture. Making learning the first priority will require radical, not incremental, changes in concepts, policies, and practices throughout the academic world. A starter solution list includes rethinking the kind of teaching that produces learning, creating consensus-based learning goals and ensuring that the undergraduate curriculum addresses all of them, implementing regular and routine assessments of learning linked to improvement strategies, demanding higher standards for and expectations of both student and faculty performance, integrating learning experiences inside and outside the classroom, revising faculty reward systems to emphasize learning and account for the value of advising and mentoring, and providing regular professional development for faculty members to strengthen teaching. These are critical steps in the right direction. The impenetrable silos of separate schools, departments, and disciplines focused first and mostly on research must yield to a broad commitment to use every institutional resource, in and out of the classroom, to promote, assess, and strengthen student learning.

Defining what is wrong helps little unless we can also determine how to make change—how to ensure that higher learning happens in higher education. To do so, we must be clear about what is required for true higher learning.

College for What?

What do we count on from colleges and universities? What do we want a college graduate to be able to do, besides list a degree on a résumé? Why, in other words, do we send two-thirds of our high school graduates to college? Is it just the next step after secondary school, or do we want something more than that? What are students supposed to get from college that they wouldn't get otherwise? Why does college matter?

One of the most common answers is that higher education should strengthen students' personal, occupational, and economic opportunity. The promise of higher education to help students make something of themselves, realize their potential, and reach their goals is itself a heartfelt expression of the American dream, and we, as a society that deeply values education, support its incarnation in community and technical colleges, public universities of all scopes and sizes, liberal arts colleges, and comprehensive research institutions. We assume that somehow the cultural pathways that lead to the American verities of individual and family economic prosperity, home ownership, and civic engagement pass directly through campus. This view is so deeply embedded and so powerful in our thinking that it can seem to be the only reason for going to college; too often, the purpose of higher education has been interpreted quite narrowly as just to get a job, or a better job. In that limited view, the change desired in students between enrollment and graduation seems only to be a shift from unemployable to employable, or, ideally, to employed.

According to a study published in 2009 by the National Center for Public Policy and Higher Education, six out of ten Americans believe colleges today are run more like businesses than campuses—zeroed in on the bottom line, rather than on students' educational experiences.[1] The pervasiveness of that mentality influences the culture and perceived priorities of higher education institutions and leads students (as it does colleges and universities) to lose sight of the higher learning they should expect. Instead, they focus on obtaining the credentials they believe will lead to employment.

Jobs are important, and every family wants their new graduate to get one; what is learned in college (which includes not just the content of academic courses, but everything else that is learned outside class) should prepare students for success after graduation. Desired college learning outcomes such as critical thinking, working in teams, and analytical reasoning are essential for many, or most, jobs. But just as a job is not the whole of a person's life, preparation for a job cannot be the whole of that person's college experience, and being ready for, or getting, a job cannot be the only reason for going to (and paying for) college.

Beyond the implied assurance of employment (a promise higher education no longer reliably keeps), the idea of positive intellectual and personal growth lies at the heart of our hopes about, goals for, and confidence in higher education. That idea distinguishes higher education in our society from primary and secondary schooling; it is what makes higher education higher—it is what puts higher learning in higher education. If we thought college was just the next mechanical, sequential step after high school, we might call it tertiary education, rather than higher education. Breaking the logic of the series of names—first primary, then secondary, then . . . higher—is no accident. The name higher education promises something extra, above and beyond. In our culture, that something extra carries significant imputed value. A college degree is supposed to signify achievement and ability that warrant not only better jobs and greater compensation, but also a special kind of respect and the recognition of added social value.

So higher education is, and is supposed to be, qualitatively different from the forms of education that came before it. And it is supposed to help students become qualitatively different—educated people—as well. The belief in that change, which is really an intentional transformation during college, means that our expectations of college are fundamentally not just about jobs and money, though jobs and money may come most quickly to mind when students and parents are asked to list the benefits of higher education. We have come to count on higher education for a more subtle, idiosyncratic, and even mysterious process of development and growth in students, something that transcends the acquisition of greater earning power and long-term increase in wealth potential: the intellectual, personal, and social emergence of a complete, adult human being. It is that transformation that truly defines the goals of higher learning. We expect colleges to change students' hearts and minds and somehow build them into whole, more mature persons; hence, we have college programs in leadership development, multicultural competency, stress management, conflict resolution, teamwork, and volunteer service, as well as academic courses and majors.

It is worth emphasizing that at its root the idea of higher learning is one of positive change: the student who graduates will not be, and should not be, the same person as the one who started college. None of the conditions of college—personal and intellectual challenge, exposure to new ideas, interactions with people who are different, the opportunity to experience new freedom and test old boundaries—are intended to leave students inert and unaffected. This is exactly what we want; at commencement, students move their tassels from one side to the other, throw their caps into the air, and greet their families after the recessional as different people.

We assume that a college graduate has become an educated person, and an educated person is both a personal and public good. We believe that the more educated our people are, and the more of our people who are educated, the better off our society will be—more secure, more stable, more prosperous, and more healthy. Accordingly, we provide generous public support to both students and colleges and universities. No other society invests in higher education as richly or consistently as we do. Perhaps no other society believes in the potential of higher education as ardently as we do.

Higher Learning

The differences that college produces should be far more meaningful and complex than just chronological growth. Students who finish college and have not changed significantly, and for the better—students who have only gotten older and taller, but not thoughtfully reassessed their perspectives or points of view, challenged their previous ways of thinking, developed greater personal and social maturity, and been prepared for the world of work and the responsibilities of citizenship—missed the opportunity that higher learning offers. And we, as a society, lost the opportunity that the development and maturation of their minds represents.

There are different kinds of learning, though we often use the word *learning* interchangeably for all of them. A student can get through college by memorizing, absorbing content knowledge in one or more fields (say history, Spanish language and literature, environmental science, mathematics, or psychology), and repeating back information given by professors convincingly enough to merit a passing grade on exams and papers. To call that process learning suggests that learning, at a very basic level, just means knowing something that you did not know before and knowing it long enough to pass the test. Things learned in such a way may, or may not, stick.

But there is a different kind of learning—the kind we should expect of higher education. Experiments in the psychology and neuroscience of learning show that learning that sticks—the kind that leads to the changes we expect of college, what we call higher learning—requires rich engagement with new material, not just memorization, and that the outcome of this engagement is a concrete and tangible change in the mind—a change in how one thinks and makes sense of the world. We see that change when students develop greater depth of understanding, can apply their new knowledge in the world, can articulate and defend a new perspective, or show new personal, social, or civic maturity. That change in the mind is not just an abstraction; we now know from brain research that learning has flesh-and-blood correlates. Advances in brain imaging allow us to "see" and measure functional and structural changes in the brain associated with learning. We change our minds because something has changed in our brains as a result of a learning experience.

Students who are seriously engaged in higher learning encounter new material—knowledge, perspectives, points of view, creations, performances, events, activities—and make sense of it in relation to their own previous knowledge, perspectives, points of view, creations, performances, events, and activities. As they continue to make connections between past knowledge and experience and new learning, the likelihood that the new learning will make sense, stick, and be available for later problem solving increases. Sometimes, processing and reflecting on the new material also inspire a significant change in capacities, attitudes, beliefs, or perspectives. "I used to think X, but, having [taken that course] [read that book] [seen that movie] [had that discussion] [done that community service project], now I think Y."

Of course none of this happens in one mighty leap; the student of the past does not become the student of the future all at once. Instead, the profound changes that make up the process of higher learning occur both predictably and unpredictably, often one at a time but sometimes in a flood, and are ordered differently for each student. But the conditions have to be right, and the student has to be engaged. Critical thinking does not emerge fully developed from one class, and the empathic ability to take the perspective of another person does not arise mechanically from a single encounter with someone unlike oneself. The changes we hope to see in students' minds and hearts are ultimately built cumulatively, gradually, and collectively from multiple intentional learning experiences inside and outside the classroom. Note that phrase, intentional learning experiences—it includes activities, from courses to volunteer service, that are designed to achieve certain desired learning outcomes. They are what a college or university can and should be accountable for creating, offering (or requiring, in many cases), providing, and assessing in an effort to support student learning, achievement, and success.

Sitting passively through college while simply finishing the growth of long bones is a waste of both individual and collective time and resources. Unfortunately, it is possible and increasingly common to do exactly that—to accumulate credit hours, meet basic academic requirements, and receive a degree without truly engaging in the process of real, substantive learning—in other words, without experiencing higher learning in higher education. Hence the phenomenon known only too well to parents, employers, and educators: that of students graduating from college, but learning little. College should be about deep, soul-searching, mind-expanding, life-enhancing learning, which may, but may not, correlate with grades, retention, and graduation. Staying in college—or, for that matter, finishing it—does not, in and of itself, signify higher learning. Persistence alone is not student success. Permitting getting through college to pass for higher learning is the great failure of higher education.

The Failure of Higher Education

There is little evidence that American higher education today promises, never mind delivers, either the educational experiences or the desired outcomes described previously. Most students graduate from college without having experienced higher learning at all—they gain (but quickly forget) factual knowledge, become adept at giving back rehearsed answers on exams, and, eventually, sporting inflated grade-point averages, find their way into line and shake hands with the president at commencement. But just accumulating credits, meeting the basic academic requirements, and picking up a diploma are poor returns on the huge investment that students, parents, and society make in higher education. Those returns seem even less attractive in the current economic climate of chronic joblessness and lingering recession. This harms not only the students and families who count on our colleges and universities to provide what Americans expect—the best higher education in the world— but also our society and our nation.

It is not surprising that an emerging and increasingly strident chorus of parents, employers, elected officials, and policy makers have begun to question the presumptive value of higher education. They complain about the high costs of college, of course, but increasingly question what really counts, the value created—or not created—by the quality and quantity of learning. Employers surveyed by the Association of American Colleges and Universities (AAC&U) have affirmed the importance of the achievement of core learning outcomes such as critical thinking among job candidates and employees, but they have also questioned the degree to which those competencies exist among today's college graduates.[2]

Decreasing public confidence in the ability of higher education to manage its own affairs and deliver on its promises has increased demands for greater institutional transparency and accountability, yet the academy remains systemically averse to making the substantial and strategic changes that would improve student learning and produce better outcomes.

Facing the possibility that higher education is failing is difficult for a country that has mostly taken for granted the quality of higher education. Efforts to improve educational systems and outcomes have almost exclusively been focused on reforms in K–12 schooling. Our nation believes in—even cherishes—higher education. We may be cynical about intellectuals, worried about how much college costs, and impatient with the hermetic unwillingness of colleges and universities to prove what they claim about student outcomes. We may complain about the inefficiencies of higher education, whisper about its hypocrisies, and snicker at its pomposity—but we deeply and fundamentally believe in the idea of higher education, and have shown an abiding faith in its quality. We as a nation have invested in that belief with money, confidence, the minds and hearts of our children, and expansive educational opportunity that has systematically removed many barriers to college admission. We have given higher education the special status that our society reserves for institutions that serve the public good—and we have assigned to it a nobility of purpose that elevates its mission and demands a kind of reverence. This reverence for higher education has been reinforced by the widely held belief that American higher education is the best in the world, a point of continuing national pride as we face inexorable global competition.

But many studies conducted over the past ten years raise serious questions about how much higher learning is taking place in higher education and suggest that our national pride in undergraduate education is less and less justified. In 2005, the Futures Project: Policy for Higher Education in a Changing World identified the expanding gap between what the public needs from higher education and how colleges and universities are serving those needs: "That gap has received little attention within institutions because they lack clear measurements for their performance and because they are satisfied with the status quo."[3] A year later, the Spellings Commission on the Future of Higher Education scathingly labeled higher education as risk aversive, self-satisfied, unduly expensive, and ineffective—characteristics that had resulted in "disturbing signs that many students who do earn degrees have not actually mastered the reading, writing, and thinking skills we expect of college graduates. Over the past decade, literacy among college graduates has actually declined. Unacceptable numbers of college graduates enter the workforce without the skills employers say they need in an economy where, as the truism holds correctly, knowledge matters more than ever."[4]

In an aptly titled book, *Academically Adrift: Limited Learning on College Campuses*, Richard Arum of New York University and Josipa Roksa of the University of Virginia document statistically insignificant gains in critical thinking, problem solving, analytical reasoning, and written communication skills; on average, there was only a 7 percent gain in these skills during the first two years of college and only marginally better when four years of study were examined.[5] Their findings are sobering: "Growing numbers of students are being sent to college at increasingly higher costs, but for a large proportion of students attending U.S. colleges the gains in critical thinking, complex reasoning and communication are either exceedingly small or empirically non-existent. At least forty-five percent of students in our sample did not demonstrate any statistically significant improvement."[6]

Corroborating data also come from the Wabash National Study of Liberal Arts Education,[7] in which students showed very modest growth on a wide range of learning outcomes; worse, some students actually regressed. Perhaps the most troubling finding in the Wabash study was that indicators of students' academic motivation showed a marked decline over their first year in college.

There is good, concrete reason then to worry about the state of undergraduate learning in higher education, not only because so little learning is taking place but also because learning seems no longer to be a high institutional priority. Arum and Roksa conclude that "there is growing evidence that individual and institutional interests and incentives are not closely aligned with a focus on undergraduate academic learning per se."[8]

Thomas Friedman coined the term "flat world" to describe the current swell of global economic, educational, and technological forces that are empowering people to "compete, connect, and collaborate" and thus equalizing opportunities for individuals worldwide.[9] What Friedman describes is more profound by far than what colleges and universities have sometimes called internationalization or globalization—words intended to convey the importance of international exchange and preparation for living and working in a globally connected world. Those concepts had more resonance before transnational competition so rapidly became the new norm; they quietly assumed that the United States would retain its first position in the global marketplace. In making his point, though, Friedman does not assume the continuation of American intellectual and economic dominance; in fact, he suggests the contrary—that we, as a society, are at real risk of losing the preeminence that has virtually defined our nation's self-image and fueled its economic growth.

This is a clear and forceful challenge to higher education: maintaining our social, economic, and intellectual leadership in a flat world. Responding effectively will require all of the intellectual horsepower and creative genius that we have traditionally associated with the best thinking, teaching, and research done in our colleges and universities. The question is not whether students graduate from college with degrees, sufficient credit hours, and networks from which they might glean their first jobs; the question is whether they graduate having learned what matters in a new world that has come rushing toward them. Can they "compete, connect, and collaborate" (to use Friedman's words) across political, cultural, and geographic boundaries? Do they have enough knowledge of self and others to be whole, moral persons who have authentic relationships and exercise solid civic commitments in a complex, diverse society? To ask the simplest questions: Are they ready? Can we rely upon them? Can we safely entrust our future to today's graduates?

In calling for "a new human capital revolution," the *New York Times* columnist David Brooks attributes high college dropout rates to the fact that students are academically unprepared and emotionally disengaged (i.e., he believes they do not drop out primarily because they are unable to afford the cost of college, as many think).[10] His speculations echo the observations and anecdotal evidence of many faculty members and administrators in higher education who see students coming to college far more intellectually and emotionally fragile than ever before and, despite their predilection for and prowess in areas such as technology, far less able to make sense of things. Stanford University psychologist William Damon worries that an increasing number of adolescents lack a sense of purpose and rather than attend college with a deliberate path, increasingly exist in college in prolonged states of "directional drift," "characterized more by indecision than by motivated reflection, more by ambivalence than by determination."[11]

The phenomenon of the helicopter parent—the mother or father who hovers and interferes in (from the college's perspective) or facilitates (from the parent's, and often the student's, perspective) their child's engagement with higher education—reflects not just a change in parental behavior, but also a parental assessment about the preparedness, resiliency, and capacity of his or her children to manage newness, complexity, and decision making for themselves. (Some developmental psychologists have proposed that college students and others in their twenties are engaged in a newly defined developmental stage called emerging adulthood, which includes the persistence of close, even dependent, relationships with parents.[12]) The larger cultural forces with which children and adolescents must cope—broken families and absentee parents, crude and violent media, economic distress, technology dependency, and the dumbing down of K–12 education—are cumulatively having adverse and perverse effects on the next generation of students prior to and during college. It ought not to come as a surprise that students suffering from directional drift attending colleges that are academically adrift end up dropping out at alarming rates and can provide or demonstrate little evidence of any serious engagement with higher education.

What Happened to Higher Learning?

To say that institutions of higher education should be concerned about learning and student success seems as obvious as saying the health care system should be concerned about health and wellness. But just as the health care system has become inflexible and unwieldy because of its emphasis on treating illness rather than promoting health, higher education has become complex and shortsighted in its emphasis on engaging in research and entrepreneurship rather than educating students, and in its assumption that teaching and learning are the same thing. Intoxicated by magazine and college-guide rankings, most colleges and universities have lost track of learning as the only educational outcome that really matters. Other priorities—higher rankings, growing enrollment, winning teams, bigger and better facilities, more revenue from sideline businesses, more research grants—have replaced learning as the primary touchstone for decision making.

Those other priorities drive institutions to divert resources from teaching and learning. For nearly all institutions, resources are not unlimited, and decisions to allocate some of them—money, people, mindshare, time, space, equipment, or land—to any one thing restricts the availability of those resources to support other things. Too many colleges and universities have chosen a dark and rocky road that leads toward a pattern of unbalanced responsiveness (which might less kindly be called obedience) to consumer demands. Note the key word *unbalanced*—we do not suggest that institutions of higher education should adopt a hermetic disinterest in the preferences and wishes of their students. But responsiveness that subjugates mission to consumer satisfaction is dangerous. Doing that nearly always results in the diversion of scarce resources to whatever it is that promises to increase a college's magazine rankings. Misguided adventures on that tortured path (especially those that involve construction or large-scale renovations and repurposing of buildings) have taken too many institutions off mission and into greater debt. Similarly, the gradual acquiescence of too many faculties and administrations to other consumer preferences—most notably lower standards for student work and classroom behavior, reduced expectations for studying and preparation outside of class, and the need for positive feedback unlinked to actual performance—deserves rigorous challenge. That long slide toward frustration can begin so subtly that no one realizes it has started, especially when its consequences (faculty expect less, so students expect less) have a certain bizarre coherence that initially suggests nothing is wrong—but it is unmistakably a critical misstep that has taken many, if not most, institutions off course.

Making the sanguine but dangerous assumption that passing grades equal learning, most colleges and universities do not adequately support, measure, or strive to improve learning itself. Most professors are not trained to teach in their graduate programs—never mind to facilitate student learning. Faculty members and administrators suffer from a common but faulty assumption that disciplinary expertise translates into teaching competency; somehow having a PhD in astrophysics or anthropology is regarded as adequate evidence of the ability to develop a course, prepare a syllabus, design and deliver lectures, create experiential learning opportunities, manage a classroom or teaching laboratory, and review and grade students' work. It isn't that most faculty members don't care about students and their learning; many do. But, given the absence of formal study in pedagogy, learning, and assessment, most professors have to learn on the job, as it were, and wide disparities in commitment and talent exist when it comes to teaching.

Other bad ideas that must have seemed good at the time, such as routinely hiring cheaper contingent or adjunct faculty to teach basic courses and permitting senior faculty to engage less with undergraduates, owe less to consumer pressure than to institutional economics (the need to save money), faculty preferences, and reward systems that privilege almost every other faculty activity over teaching, advising, and mentoring undergraduates. The idea of saving money by hiring cheaper contingent faculty members, to whom no long-term commitments are made and for whom no benefits are usually provided, betrays a belief that teaching is a low-priority activity and suggests that it doesn't much matter who teaches undergraduates—especially when teaching is not evaluated anyway. Even where teaching has a defined value in the evaluation and advancement of faculty members, there is usually little, if any, attention to the quality or quantity of student learning attributable to the faculty member's work. The consequences of these policies and practices for undergraduate education are severe, and the gradual disappearance of full-time and tenure-track professors from lower division courses and student life calls loudly for a reassessment of priorities.

Few institutions are diligent about assessing student learning, and fewer still use the results of such assessments to improve learning experiences or determine professional development needs for faculty members. Yet, the assessment of learning is an indispensable way not primarily or solely of holding the academy fiscally or politically accountable, but of truly ensuring high-quality learning in college—a form of learning that justifies the term higher education. Assessment should not be an afterthought or an add-on intended to satisfy some requirement; it is the only way to tell whether learning experiences of all kinds achieve their purposes.

The effects of the loss of focus, emphasis, and priority on learning in higher education are easy to discern and describe. Baccalaureate degrees have become basic commodities, purchased like other consumer goods. The degree has been cheapened by letting it certify only the process of going through the motions of college.

Degrees as Deliverables

Trends such as unbalanced or obsequious responsiveness to consumer demands (especially at the expense of mission and standards), the increasingly widespread use of cheaper ways to "teach" more undergraduates, and any strategy derived from a narrow focus on costs rather than value (which leads inexorably to proposals to reinvent higher education by implementing various economic and educational shortcuts such as three-year bachelor's degrees) reflect a more general and serious problem: the assumption that the purpose of colleges and universities—the mission of higher education—is to award degrees. The idea that a degree must be earned, not just awarded, seems antiquated and rustic when students and parents, thinking like consumers, assume that a degree is the natural, not-to-be-questioned, routine and regular deliverable of colleges and universities. If a degree is simply a deliverable, purchased by the payment of tuition and fees, the importance of requirements that must be met and assessment of performance against some kind of standard is seriously diminished. If a degree is a deliverable, then colleges and universities, working according to sound business practices and principles, should erect as few barriers as possible to both entry (admission) and exit (the degree). Standards? Speed bumps. Three-year degrees? Of course; why not? How efficient!

After all, why else would anyone go to college, except to get a degree? Why else would parents pay tens of thousands of dollars for their sons and daughters to have four, five, or six of the best years of their lives? What responsible consumer would shell out that kind of money if the outcome were uncertain? We speak often of tuition and fees as investments in the future; what possible return do they offer if not a degree?

That is the worst of the bad ideas that are ruining American undergraduate higher education: that one goes to college to get a degree; that the degree is the deliverable from a college; that students deserve the degree if they have put in their time, paid their tuition, gone to their classes, accumulated their credits, and gotten passing grades in enough courses. In the service of that very bad idea and the assumptions and values that support and surround it, we base our assessments of students' work in college on plain numerical metrics, such as grade point averages and credit hours. Nothing in that schema suggests that learning is a goal; passing, staying in school, and getting enough credits to graduate are the goals. Graduating is important, but focusing on "completion," to use a term that has become popular in today's discussions of higher education, makes sense only if completion is defined by achieving learning goals and acquiring desired competencies. The sad truth is that while it is possible to get a liberal education without earning a degree, it is also possible to earn a degree without getting a liberal education. In America today, higher education is using the wrong touchstone for decision making.

The touchstone for decision making has become not learning, but throughput: getting enough students recruited, admitted, enrolled, retained, and graduated—that is, giving people degrees. Let not the faculty get in the way of the smooth operation of that system as it processes students from inquiry to commencement along a flowchart designed by enrollment management and alumni relations. Let not alleged standards and community expectations for student behavior prevail over the need to keep students earning credit hours. Let not some irascible professor halt progress because of a concern about plagiarism or other academic misconduct. Bad grades and unfortunate judicial actions or sanctions are the enemy of throughput—which means that high expectations inside or outside the classroom only create friction in the machinery.

When throughput rules, institutional accountability is measured by comparative benchmarks, almost all of them quantitative, rather than qualitative—the number and test scores of students admitted, levels of tuition and other revenue, library holdings, technology, endowment per student, class sizes, reputation-based ranking, levels of funding for research programs, and scholarly publications—not what and how well students learn. Institutional change is concerned with enhancing reputation, rather than with improving learning. Improvements are made for stardom in rankings in the popular press.

When we understand that the touchstone for decision making is throughput, the priorities, strategies, goals, and decisions of colleges and universities are much more straightforward to figure out. Why would a college spend a lot of money on the complex, interrelated academic and support services needed to reduce premature departure from school and promote learning and student success?

Process or Outcome: Teaching or Learning?

Most colleges and universities today view teaching and learning through a conceptual lens that sees them as one and the same. Using that lens, institutions of higher education assume the following: if teaching occurs, learning happens. This is a precariously romantic and utterly ungrounded assumption that suggests that the purpose of colleges and universities is to teach. We argue that the actual purpose of higher education is for students to learn. Teaching and learning are not the same thing.

The flawed but unfortunately ubiquitous and historically unquestioned belief in teaching among colleges and universities was forcefully identified more than a decade ago by Robert Barr and John Tagg, who called for a fundamental paradigm shift in higher education: "Now, however, we are beginning to recognize that our dominant paradigm mistakes a means for an end. It takes the means or method—called 'instruction' or 'teaching' and makes it the college's end or purpose. To say that the purpose of colleges is to provide instruction is like saying that General Motors' business is to operate assembly lines or that the purpose of medical care is to fill hospital beds. We now see that our mission is not instruction but rather that of producing learning with every student by whatever means work best."[13]

We are not suggesting that there is no relationship between teaching and learning. It is often true, as Ralph Waldo Emerson once noted, that "the ends reside in the means"; teaching and learning are distinct, yet inextricably connected. But one should not be mistaken for the other because one is not the same as, or equal to, the other. Ineffective professors can teach for years; their students may learn little or nothing from them. Teaching is the process through which pedagogy delivers content in one or another kind of learning experience; learning is, as we have noted earlier, a change in the learner produced by engagement with learning experiences. They are related, but not identical; either one can occur without the other.

But institutions of higher education continue mistakenly to see, and treat, teaching and learning as equivalent, and in doing so perpetuate systems, policies, and practices that reinforce a skewed culture, constantly undermining the stated mission of learning. These systems, policies, and practices include the training of professors as researchers and scholars, but not as teachers; faculty incentive and reward systems that recognize teaching, but not learning; the assessment of teaching, not student learning and achievement; and a conception of accountability based on inputs such as admissions selectivity and the ratio of faculty members to students, not the achievement of actual, demonstrable new knowledge, skills, commitments, or competencies among students. Professors do not fail to achieve promotion and tenure because their students did not learn; in fact, few colleges and universities know to what extent, if at all, any professors' students have learned or not. In many universities, for that matter, professors do not fail to achieve promotion and tenure because they do not teach well, either.

How did such an educational worldview develop, and how does it remain so potent? It begins with faculty and administrators, who, having attained their scholarly degrees under a similar educational regime, see themselves as consummately successful learners who are, by virtue of their disciplinary expertise, sufficiently well prepared to teach. Given their successful academic experience, the endorsement of teaching versus learning that they receive from their campus culture, and their lack of training in teaching or learning, most faculty members inevitably acquire a teaching-centric view of higher education. They believe, albeit naively, that their students are or should be equally motivated and able to learn in a fashion similar to the way in which they did, or think they did. The assumption is self-referenced: my students are like me and can and will learn the way I did. Viewed through the scholar/teacher's lens, knowledge itself is seen as supreme; to know your discipline is to be able to teach it, and transferring such knowledge to students, whose job it is to receive and accurately feed it back to you on papers and examinations, is the desired achievement of a professor.

In this prevailing teaching-centric worldview, colleges take responsibility for delivering instruction through courses, programs, and teaching, with students being held solely responsible for learning. That is, the institution does not hold itself accountable for whether students learn, only for ensuring that faculty members provide teaching and instruction. This perspective sees a university as a kind of bank with intellectual assets that are available to students, but it is entirely the students' responsibility to identify, qualify, and use those assets effectively.

The assumptions underlying this view are both distressing and obvious. In the first place, only the student bears responsibility for learning and for linking or integrating learning that occurs (if it does) in various learning activities and experiences. The job of faculty members is just to put it out there, delivering the content of a course, for example, in X number of class sessions and assignments over Y period of weeks. Since teaching is the work of professors, it is also assumed that learning takes place primarily (or only) in classrooms and teaching laboratories, as though students turn off their ability to learn as they leave the room when class ends. Therefore, whatever students learn outside classrooms is by definition less important than what is taught in classrooms, and the connection between the two, if made at all, must be engineered by the student. Note that few, if any, students fail to graduate because they did not make these connections. For that matter, note also that few, if any, colleges and universities assess whether or not students made those connections.

Since teaching is what matters and what is measured, instruction is mostly lecture-driven and learning, to the extent that it occurs, is mostly a passive, receptive enterprise. In other words, students should come to class, listen carefully, take good notes, and be grateful. Expectations and standards of excellence for students are too often quite low; meeting them requires minimal student (and faculty) effort. But grades are high; the phenomenon of grade inflation is a mutually beneficial accommodation between students who do not want to invest much time in learning and faculty members who do not want to invest much time in teaching, supported by the influence of many parents, who are often more interested in degrees than learning. When teaching is the focus, assessment primarily takes place at the end of the class, course, or other teaching activity, through the imposition of grades (and, sometimes, of course and/or professor evaluations). Generally, any such assessment happens too late to permit any revision of teaching, not to mention learning, strategies.

The educational outputs of this teaching-centric view are damaging: a large percentage of what students have learned vanishes after the grades are in; almost half of students who begin college never finish;[14] and the results of national tests of college student achievement have been dismal for years. Worse, these data are largely ignored by leaders in positions to respond and instigate reform.

In contrast, the kind of higher learning we advocate and described earlier in this chapter requires that students be fully engaged participants in a powerful intellectual, social, and developmental process. That process requires rigorous self-discipline, effort, and commitment; demanding, well-trained teachers; an inspiring, motivating, and diverse curriculum; and an intentionally designed, challenging, formative, and supportive learning environment. It is a kind of learning that requires the attainment of substantial knowledge, conceptual understanding, critical thinking, writing and speaking skills, various ways of knowing, compassion, moral integrity, and a genuine sense of humility.

The bad news is that few colleges and universities today operate according to those principles. The good news is that much research supports such learning and begs for a reorientation of higher education towards a learning-centric model. In such a model, students indeed take responsibility for their learning by investing adequate time, effort, and motivation, but effective, successful learning is not their responsibility alone. Achievement is a responsibility that must be shared by faculty and staff who embrace an alternative set of learning principles. We note those principles briefly here and will expand upon them later in this book:

- Higher learning requires the collective effort of the entire faculty and staff—a purposeful sharing of ends (e.g., well-rounded knowledge as well as core competencies and skills, such as critical thinking, perspective taking, and writing) and means, such that students are expected, for example, to engage in rigorous thinking, reading, writing, and ethical behavior in every class.
- Higher learning occurs horizontally, across experiences in and out of the classroom, as well as vertically within majors and disciplines, and in ways that are necessarily cumulative. This properly suggests that the whole is greater than the sum of its parts—that higher learning is not simply incremental and additive, but is in fact synergistic and requires mindful, coherent, and integrated design.
- Students are intentionally thrown off balance through the creation of what psychologists label cognitive disequilibrium, as a way of forcing students to question what they think they know and understand and to differentiate that from what they have been told was true.
- Assessment is, first and foremost, an intentional process of helping students learn, including how to seek, use, and internalize assessment processes and results. It helps students develop an ability to evaluate their own work, sources of information, the quality of knowledge, and the work of others. It is how institutions judge curricular and teaching effectiveness.
- All learning—intellectual, developmental, social, and emotional— happens through changes in the microscopic anatomy and function of the brain. Multidisciplinary research and strong collaboration

among neuroscientists, cognitive psychologists, and educators are increasingly able to provide helpful guidance in developing policies, practices, and pedagogies that help students learn more effectively.

- The individual learner matters in the learning. Learners may be differently equipped to learn on any given day, in a specific context, and at a particular time. Students' readiness to learn is a complex construct that influences persistence, achievement, learning, and success. Students' readiness to learn must be a fundamental concern of all institutions of higher education.
- Students' individual levels of engagement and investment in their college education are also fundamental factors that affect achievement, persistence, and success.

Viewing higher education through a learning-centric lens, one cannot escape seeing that it is the learner and the learning that matter. With these alternative principles as our foundation, we need to initiate a national conversation with and about our colleges and universities. From such alternative principles and the reconsidered curricula and renewed learning environments that spring from them, we can begin to engage students in the kind of learning that justifies the term higher learning. Sound evidence from research on the brain, developmental learning, teaching, assessment, and institutional change supports this fundamental shift in our perspective from teaching to learning. It is to those topics that we now turn.

Conclusion

Many well-intentioned analyses and critiques of the problems of higher education have focused on access, cost, retention, and accountability, all of which are important in their own right, but ultimately improving those problems would not correct the core deficits in the quality of learning. To provide excellent, transformative learning for students, institutions must themselves be culturally transformed. The solutions are not a mystery, but they are not the usual ones—just providing more funding or adding more technology, for example, will not alone suffice. What is required is change in the entrenched attitudes, priorities, and cultures of colleges and universities; we must challenge watered-down undergraduate curricula, ineffective teaching methods, and the lowered expectations and standards that reduce students to passive consumers, demanding little of themselves or their institutions and expecting to be spoon-fed rather than required to actively engage in an education that is both demanding and transforming.

Research on learning, organizational development, and institutional experience offers the fundamentals of the much-needed reforms: publicly acknowledging there is a problem, shifting priorities from research to valuing and assessing learning, appreciating that higher learning is cumulative and thus involves the collective efforts of the faculty, intentionally engaging students inside and outside the classroom, making curricula far more coherent and rigorous, demanding and supporting far greater student effort in learning, and significantly raising expectations and standards while simultaneously using timely and appropriate feedback provided by assessment to improve learning.

We are calling for a change in the academy's culture—not just incremental steps and fine adjustments that leave the basic assumptions, priorities, and methods of higher education untouched. What needs rethinking is the quality of higher education itself. The best research on institutional change confirms that institutional culture change requires a combination of grassroots and senior-level leadership, evidence-based decision making, and strong institutional will. Overcoming resistance to change in our colleges and universities, especially in the competitive environment of higher education today, requires change in our larger culture as well; we need a powerful wave of new, higher expectations and reordered priorities washing across our campuses.

This is an emergency. We have already waited too long to start this conversation. Our analysis and discourse must go beyond the narrow, predictable questions of retention and price inflation in higher education to focus on mission—not simply graduation rates, costs, or three-year degrees. Access, persistence, retention, and graduation are all important, but the crisis in student learning is the real issue. This is where the big gaps are; this is where too many colleges and universities fail to deliver what they promise. Reversing this failure will require substantial institutional renewal and a new national commitment to reinstate higher learning in undergraduate education.

2

Judging College Quality

Claiming Quality in Undergraduate Education

While American universities still set the world standard for research, the same cannot be said for their stature in undergraduate education. In fact, there is disturbing and consistent evidence that our colleges and universities no longer provide the quality of undergraduate learning that this nation needs and should rightly demand. As this deficiency grows and is more widely recognized and discussed, we witness both increasingly strident critiques and declining public support.

Few weeks go by without the publication of new studies by federal agencies or think tanks, scholarly articles, or whole books that assail the policies, practices, inefficiencies, or poor outcomes of higher education.[1] And yet—in a remarkable challenge to the usual economic principles that explain consumer behavior—both demand and prices continue to rise. American students, their families, and lenders of all types complain about the increasing cost of going to college, but year after year those costs grow—and we continue to pay them. So generations of students graduate from college with degrees that have far less measurable and undisputed value than the debt they have accumulated to earn them. Students who graduated in 2009 and borrowed money to cover their college costs had an average of about $24,000 in student loan debt, according to the Project on Student Debt.[2] Loan payments will continue to be due long after graduation.

All of which prompts a question about our "elite" institutions: What makes an undergraduate education at any American college or university worth a price of $35,000–$55,000 a year? And then there is an even more difficult question: How much better is the education at an elite private college that costs $50,000 a year than it is at another institution, public or private, that charges far less—perhaps $5,000–$15,000? Not to mention the hardest questions: What, exactly, do students get for that money (whether it is $5,000 or $55,000)? Or, what does college deliver in return for an average of $24,000 in indebtedness for student loans at graduation?

These are not hypothetical questions. They are commonly raised at admission gatherings for prospective students and their anxious, checkbook-conscious parents. But what are the answers? Let's start with the question about the value of education at an institution that charges $25,000, $30,000, $35,000, $40,000, $45,000, or even more in tuition and required fees. The responses one hears are so standard and rehearsed that they are almost liturgical. Presidents, vice presidents, deans, and directors of admissions at schools that charge tuition and fees at those levels all say some narrow variation of the same things. "It's worth it because" begins a sequence of claims about high retention and graduation rates, high levels of student satisfaction and happiness, greater selectivity in admissions, excellent (and often new) facilities, small class sizes, and desirable faculty-to-student ratios.

All of those metrics are, of course, the heart and soul of college rankings in magazines as well (along with measures of racial diversity, amounts of research funding and numbers of scholarly publications by faculty members, and student and alumni ratings of everything from the quality of food to the level of pride in the institution). But note that the numbers reported for those metrics on any campus mean something only in comparison to the numbers being reported on other campuses. Colleges often refer to them as benchmarks, but benchmarks are not standards; they are just reference points selected by colleges to support comparisons among institutions. The measured and reported levels of student satisfaction with educational programs or student services on one campus may not mean anything, other than that those levels are higher or lower than what is found at some competing institution—and, unless the two institutions use exactly the same survey instrument and conduct their research in exactly the same ways, the results may not be comparable anyway. We don't know what the ideal levels of satisfaction or students' happiness or the ideal faculty-to-student ratio or average class size actually are.

We don't know what these numbers mean even on any specific campus, never mind whether that meaning translates from campus to campus. So the recitations of speakers at those admissions events come down to this: "We have more of this, or less of that, than some range of other schools, so we cost more." "Trust me on this," they might add.

If magazine rankings and the simple quantitative metrics that fuel them told us how much and how well students learned, we would have little quarrel with them. But they tell us no such thing. No president is going to stand before prospective students and their parents and say, "We cost more because we spend a lot of money on things that will make us look better in the rankings," or "You pay more here because we turn ourselves inside out making your student happy and satisfied here." If only happiness and satisfaction correlated with learning! One long-serving college president said to us, "Happy, happy, happy! Isn't there something more than happy?"

The next logical question, then, is this: What evidence is there that students learn more, or better, at this college? On the rare occasions when that question is actually asked, quite a painful, long, and awkward pause usually follows. Then there are either blustery reassurances untroubled by data or soaring allusions to tradition, sometimes laced with the names of famous and allegedly well-educated alumni, living or dead. The generosity and politeness of listeners, combined with the aura created by quickly spoken words that always seem to sound good, usually prevent anyone from asking the natural follow-up question: "So there isn't evidence that the quality of learning here is any better than it is anywhere else?" or the even more distressing follow-up query, "Which means we can't be sure what we're paying for, right?"

Is quality in undergraduate education mostly a matter of faith? Do we just trust, data and other evidence aside and notwithstanding, that any particular college provides a good education? The most honest answer is a regretful "Yes." Until relatively recently, estimates of college quality have been essentially "faith based" because there has been little direct or reliable evidence of how any given school contributes to students' learning. This situation has forced parents and students alike to take a leap of faith that all the money they pay, all the loans they endure, all the sacrifices they make to send their student to an expensive college, and all the educational and other experiences their student has in college will somehow pay off. How could they not believe that? After all, this college has a higher faculty-to-student ratio and a smaller average class size than other schools . . . and, besides, there are all these new buildings, and look at that climbing wall! You can get almost anything you want in the food court, too. If only some of those qualities correlated with learning.

But as has happened with other faith-based American institutions and shibboleths, faith without works no longer suffices. Consider health care: who, even twenty years ago, would have predicted the fast and amazing demise of the comforting cultural image of the selfless, caring physician—or the striking loss of public confidence in health care in general? Or churches: while it is undoubtedly true that most priests, ministers, rabbis, and other religious authorities are ethical, moral people of principle, we are no longer surprised by new revelations of shameful conduct by their less principled colleagues. The list goes on—investment banking, hedge funds, energy companies, and government agencies and officials. Now we, the public, are asking more and more difficult questions and refusing to accept faith-based answers about higher education as well. What are students learning?

Answers based on evidence are scarce, and few institutions of higher education have consented to having whatever data they have about student learning compared in any public way with data from other institutions—especially their competitors. This lack of systematically collected, compared, and reported data on student learning from American colleges and universities caused the Spellings Commission on the Future of Higher Education, appointed by the secretary of education in George W. Bush's presidency, to conclude that there is a "remarkable absence of accountability mechanisms . . . leaving all to wonder which institutions do a better job than others of not only graduating students but of actually teaching them something."[3]

In *Measuring Up 2008: The National Report Card on Higher Education*, the National Center for Public Policy and Higher Education noted the lack of progress on benchmarks of student learning. After awarding no grade to any state on this element of the report card—"All states receive an 'Incomplete' in Learning because there are not sufficient data to allow meaningful state-by-state comparisons"[4]—the center provided the following stark analysis: "As in 2000, there are still no common benchmarks that would permit state comparisons of the knowledge and skills of college students. There are isolated instances in which learning outcomes are assessed, such as South Dakota's mandatory exam of rising college juniors. But there is no nationwide approach to assessing learning that would allow state-to-state comparisons. What energy was available for state assessments in 2000 has been directed to campus-level assessments in 2008, such as the Voluntary System of Accountability. This represents a step backward, not forward."[5]

The few comparative data points we do have—such as average SAT and ACT scores for entering students, four- or six-year graduation rates, faculty salaries, and levels of alumni giving, all of those magazine metrics—do not predict the impact of any college on learning. Sadly, they also do not predict the likelihood of a graduate's getting a job or being paid a certain starting salary. These metrics turn out not to have much more value than the percentage of residence hall rooms that are air conditioned or the number of useable square feet in the recreation center. So what is the prize for getting into the "right" college? And how can one tell what the "right" college is?

Four Ways of Judging College Quality

There are four usual ways of judging college quality: actuarial data, expert ratings, student/alumni surveys, and the direct assessment of student performance.[6] Colleges and universities generally rely on the first three of these measures because the data that inform them are typically easy and inexpensive to collect and are readily available—not because they actually tell us what we need to know about the quality or quantity of student learning. The first three trip off the tongues of college officials and administrators as they try to convince prospects and parents that their institution is worth all that money. They comprise the easily packaged quantifiable information—retention rates, average class sizes, endowment per student, presidential rankings—frequently cited in the media and enthusiastically reported in college and university press releases, used *ad nauseam* in the magazine rankings, trumpeted in institutional marketing materials, and selectively (but attractively) displayed on websites. Though these measurements are easy to gather and have long been assumed to indicate or serve as proxy measures for institutional quality, there is little evidence that they tell us anything whatsoever about quality in terms of learning or student outcomes.

Many colleges also use standardized surveys to get students to report their own personal assessments of various aspects and components of their college experiences. The National Survey of Student Engagement (NSSE), the most popular and highly regarded of these instruments, has been administered at more than six hundred colleges and universities.[7] Students respond to a (long) series of questions about things such as the quantity and quality of contact with the faculty and how much homework, reading, and writing they actually do—all of which are commonly used markers of levels of engagement. While it is undoubtedly true that some of those factors are associated with learning, none of them is a direct measure, and none by itself has been shown to predict learning. It is hard to imagine that students would learn very much without spending time on homework, for example, but spending time on homework won't assure learning. NSSE scores may be a more useful measurement of how well schools teach than many of the other metrics that find their way into the college rankings, but correlation isn't causation. Thus surveys like the NSSE offer, at best, an indirect assessment of educational quality by focusing only on teaching and student activities. They do not directly assess student learning, and they cannot recognize or measure the transformative process that higher learning inspires.

The fourth and last way to assess college quality is the important, regular evaluation of student performance. This takes place in classrooms on all college campuses, including the virtual classrooms of online universities, and results in the assignment of grades and the calculation of grade point averages (GPAs). There is, unfortunately, no absolute standard for either one; an A on one campus may indicate about as much achievement as a C on another. For that matter, an A in a political science course may have little correlation with a similar grade in an economics course in the same college. And the differences between an A– and a B+ are so subtle they often are meaningless. The problem is that in most circumstances the only standard available for grading is that of the individual professor. Different professors—on one campus as well as across many campuses—have different standards, expectations, and degrees of exactness and precision in grading. Ultimately, grades have become a cultural phenomenon defined and understood differently in each department and college. When degrees are understood and treated as deliverables and commodities, grading must be approached in such a way as to remove, rather than create, barriers to graduation.

More importantly, an A by itself tells us little about how well a student retains the knowledge and cognitive skills and tools gleaned from a specific course, or about students' ability to apply newly acquired knowledge and skills in novel situations. Of equal importance, grades do not capture the collective and cumulative effects of dozens of courses over a four-, five-, or six-year stretch—nor do they document the educational and life experiences happening outside the classroom that supplement and enrich learning during college.

So grades have become poor indicators of educational quality, just as have the actuarial measures described earlier. Grade inflation—the nearly universal consequence of the marriage of declining standards with consumer values—has rendered GPAs so unreliable and suspect that some corporate recruiters have begun to ask interviewees for their SAT scores instead. Think about what that means! It says that some recruiters now believe that standardized data about the educational aptitude of entering students (for instance, SAT or ACT scores) are more predictive of success on the job than unstandardized, culturally constructed, poorly correlated data about academic performance in college. Grades then tell us practically nothing—a reality noted by the Middle States Commission on Higher Education, one of the major accrediting bodies for colleges and universities. The commission's following statement cleanly disposes of grades as a reliable indicator of learning: "Grades are not direct evidence of student learning . . . a grade alone does not express the content of what a student has learned . . . only the degree to which the student is perceived to have learned in a specific context."[8]

So what then do grades actually show? Grades primarily show the degree to which students have been successful in anticipating and meeting a professor's requirements for the display of knowledge that was intended to be acquired in a course. Cramming the night before a midterm or final exam installs enough facts in short-term memory to allow clever and high-functioning students to pass (or, in too many colleges, to even get A's and B's). But higher learning depends far less on short-term memorization of information than on the integration of knowledge and the generation of meaning by each student—processes that require time, reflection, and feedback. So it is that a student can ace an exam, or a course, without having learned anything of substance; the hastily memorized facts and figures fade quickly from the mind, leaving little evidence that anything there has changed. But if grades do not suffice in demonstrating learning, how do we know that learning has happened? How can colleges prove that their educational programs are effective?

In other chapters of this book, we make the case that higher learning is a collective, cumulative process in which students advance toward the achievement of desired learning goals through the aggregate influence and agency of many intentional learning experiences that occur throughout the undergraduate experience, inside and outside the classroom. Students do not develop the ability to think critically and solve problems, for example, as a result of any single course or experiential learning activity; mastering critical thinking and problem solving skills and learning to write accurately and well require much practice and feedback over time. To make that approach to learning possible, faculty members must reach consensus on desired cross-disciplinary learning goals and ensure that those goals are addressed in their courses through careful design of syllabi, communication with students about the learning to be achieved, the use of sound pedagogy, and diligent and frequent formative and summative assessment. Similarly, learning experiences inside and outside the classroom must be coupled tightly, through partnerships between faculty and student affairs professionals (the nonfaculty professional staff members who provide out-of-class experiential learning opportunities and manage student academic and personal support services, such as personal counseling, health services, and residence life programs), so that the goals, achievement, and assessment of learning across the entire college experience are made a coherent whole.

The problem is that few institutions have achieved, or have tried to achieve, such coherence. In particular, there is little measurement of cumulative, collective student learning—not to mention the absence of the necessary consensus among faculty members to define learning goals and the limited, mostly unsustained nature of partnerships with student affairs professionals that would provide the essential framework for defining and meeting common learning goals. Professors care deeply about whether students learn what is taught in their courses, but a lack of consensus within and across disciplines usually prevents agreement among them on cumulative and collective learning goals. And where consensus has been reached about institutional goals and objectives such as critical thinking, ethical and moral development, and global awareness, the level of abstraction required to achieve agreement renders them vacuous. Without clear delineation of those goals, it is difficult to create reliable and consistent measures of student learning—especially measures that might be used to make comparisons of the effectiveness of different institutions.

It is not that the attempt to define and install such measures has never been made. There has been significant resistance to developing such measures—and, more generally, to the assessment of learning itself—within institutions for several reasons. Attempts to institute mechanical, template-driven, or formulaic systems of assessment of student learning—based primarily on attempts to demonstrate that students have acquired new capacities and competencies, without accommodating differences among disciplines and ways of knowing—have certainly inspired resistance and inflamed tempers. It is fair to say that the assessment of learning in the humanities will be different from that done in the social or natural sciences—except when the desired learning being assessed is in the broad category of cumulative and collective learning (such as analytical reasoning, problem solving, quantitative literacy, and writing). Philosophers and physicists might assess students' progress toward proficiency in problem solving in similar ways using different material, but the philosophy professor and his physicist colleague will each use very different ways of assessing serious, thoughtful, reflective learning (the kind of learning that qualifies as higher learning, which requires meaning making, as opposed to memorization and just-in-time ingestion of facts) in their own disciplines. The failure to accommodate such necessary and appropriate pluralism in assessing learning across a variety of disciplines has undermined the acceptance, adoption, and implementation of learning assessments in many institutions.

In addition, some faculty members and administrators assert that it is difficult or impossible to measure important learning and/or that learning only becomes evident long after the undergraduate years have ended (when assessments done during college cannot observe and capture it). Armed with colloquialisms such as "If you can measure it, it doesn't matter" and "If it matters, you can't measure it," faculty and academic administrators who hold those points of view have vigorously defended traditional grading as a valid assessment of learning in classes, courses, general education, and the majors. They also have questioned the need for and the validity of any other means of assessing learning. The effect of these arguments is to create a kind of nihilism about learning assessments that has been difficult for assessment advocates to challenge successfully.

Other professors and academic administrators see the assessment of learning as yet another unfunded mandate forced upon them. Some fear that any kind of assessment not of their own making is a threat to academic freedom. While many faculty members are enthusiastic about the possibility that assessment, rightly applied, can improve learning, others see it as an oppressive tool of administrators (and, sometimes, legislators) who seek to micromanage instruction, impose their own agenda, and/ or curry favor with voters by claiming to have brought accountability to higher education. Even faculty members whose attitudes toward the assessment of learning are warmer and more positive face the challenge of learning how to do such assessments well; few institutions have provided the professional development experiences and resources needed to help professors be successful in this endeavor.

The discouraging bottom line is just this: three of the four ways of judging college quality do not correlate with learning at all, and the fourth—regular evaluation of student performance—has been primarily used to give grades, not to assess learning. It is therefore not yet possible to substitute evidence-based assessments of the quality and quantity of learning for today's faith-based, rankings-oriented approach.

A Crisis of Low Expectations

Tom Wolfe, the noted author, essayist, and chronicler of American cultural shifts over the past forty years, offered a harsh judgment of universities and the undergraduate learning environment in *I Am Charlotte Simmons*, a novel published in 2004.[9] Wolfe is an extraordinary narrator; in this story of an innocent encountering the complexities of college, he illuminates the debilitating impact of collegiate social and cultural norms concerning sexual behavior, alcohol abuse, and athletic privilege—all unchecked, he notes, by academic or intellectual challenge.

He sums up his observations by asking, "All those boys and girls . . . do parents—does anybody—have any idea what happens to them in college?"[10] Barrett Seaman answers this question in his aptly titled book, *Binge: Campus Life in an Age of Disconnection and Access*, the product of two years of immersion research about undergraduate life and experience on 12 highly regarded campuses. Students on our most privileged campuses, he found, grapple mostly with personal, psychological, and relational issues and concerns—casual and ambiguous social relationships, anxiety and depression, racial tension, interpersonal conflicts—rather than academic or intellectual ones. "Classes have their place in the calendar of events. As far as I can see, however, the drama of daily life revolves around clubs and teams and the getting and spending of social capital—the essence of the undergraduate experience," he notes.[11] At the center of this life, he finds the widespread use of alcohol to be "dangerously unchecked."

We use alcohol abuse only as an example; it is just one facet of an institutional culture among traditional-age undergraduates that has gone off track, but it illustrates the more general problem of low expectations in college. Going to a strange town and getting drunk every night is an image of college that none of us wants to accept, but the quotation resonates in many ways. In today's undergraduate college culture, high-risk drinking—long regarded, with good reason, as the dominant campus public health concern[12]—persists despite the serious efforts of health educators, administrators, clinicians, researchers, and public health practitioners. While many factors contribute to the sustainability of high-risk drinking, especially among traditional-age undergraduates and on residential campuses, one especially important contributor is low expectations about both personal and professional, or academic, behavior. The mantra "work hard, party hard" obscures the fact that too many students are not actually working very hard at all. Since high-risk drinking affects not only students' health, safety, and relationships, but also their memory, learning, and academic performance, it is a profoundly mission-central concern for colleges and universities. High standards for both personal and academic performance that inherently require substantially more student time and effort studying might challenge students enough to make being drunk less likely, less attractive, and less culturally resonant and rewarded. But neither faculty members nor their

more advanced student peers any longer create expectations of significant academic workloads in the minds of entering freshmen. "Academ-
ics," as many student admissions tour guides call activities associated
with learning and the educational program during those promotional
campus tours on which they walk backwards in order to point out the
sights along the way, can be covered without too much interference in
social life and parties.

For many undergraduates, it is in fact possible to get by academically
without working very hard. Low academic expectations have become the
accepted norm in campus life.[13] NSSE data and other studies show that
on average undergraduate students are doing a mere 10 to 15 hours per
week of homework while receiving grades of B or higher in their courses.
Seniors spend the same amount of time studying as freshmen. Students
at all levels report little demand for writing—50 percent of seniors report
not writing a paper longer than 20 pages in their last year of college.[14]
A recent study of student effort in the University of California system
amplifies these data; its students averaged 11.5 hours of homework per
week in the social sciences, 11.9 hours per week in the arts and humanities, and 15.1 hours in sciences and engineering.[15] Similarly, the Center
for Studies in Education at the University of California–Berkeley points
out that in 1961, the average college student spent 24 hours per week
studying, while current students spend only a little more than half that
time. This precipitous decline is well documented for all demographic
subgroups, all majors, all levels of institutional selectivity, and regardless
of whether students hold jobs while in school. The Center for Studies in
Higher Education report concludes, "The most plausible explanation for
these findings is . . . that standards have fallen at postsecondary institutions in the United States."[16]

Leon Botstein, the president of Bard College, asserts that even on the
most elite campuses—where presumably the ethos of idealism, ambi-
tion, commitment, and hard work is emphasized, more often than not—
students are asked for little and give little in return. This tacit *folie a deux*
can be engaged and reinforced in classroom, residential, experiential
learning, and volunteer service activities. Free time too often gets filled
by extracurricular activities in which students display "aspects of anti-
intellectualism that directly contradict and undermine stated academic
ideals and intentions," Botstein writes.[17] Faculty and administrators, he

says, are complicit in and share in the responsibility and accountability for perpetuating this campus culture; students could not have created and sustained it by themselves.[18]

A Growing Consensus on Institutional Ineffectiveness

The findings from the 2004 *National Report Card on Higher Education* condemn the work and outcomes of our colleges and universities, calling higher education's lack of effectiveness "a wake-up call for our country . . . the inescapable fact is that America is underperforming in higher education."[19] Derek Bok, former president of Harvard, having spent several years reviewing the evidence on college effectiveness, concurs; too much learning is left incomplete, a judgment echoed in his book's title: *Our Underachieving Colleges: A Candid Look at How Much Students Learn and Why They Should Be Learning More.*[20]

The Association of American Colleges and Universities (AAC&U), a leading professional organization in higher education that represents more than a thousand institutional members from the full spectrum of American colleges and universities—concluded in its landmark study of undergraduate quality, *Greater Expectations: A New Vision for Learning as a Nation Goes to College*, that the situation is urgent, because "even as college attendance is rising, the performance of too many students is faltering. [College] is a revolving door for millions of students while the college years are poorly spent by many others."[21] The American Council of Trustees and Alumni, having done its own study, pointed to the institutions' lack of intellectual rigor and failure to require fundamental coursework in history, science, literature, and mathematics. In its evaluation of general education requirements in one hundred leading colleges and universities, the council awarded 60 percent of them grades of C, D, and F. The council concluded the following about its findings: "What we found is alarming. Even as our students need broad-based skills and knowledge to succeed in the global marketplace, our colleges and universities are failing to deliver. Topics like U.S. government or history, literature, mathematics, and economics have become mere options on far too many campuses. Not surprisingly, students are graduating with great gaps in their knowledge—and employers are noticing. If not remedied, this will have significant consequences for U.S. competitiveness and innovation."[22]

The few available studies that directly measure college learning (as noted earlier, the elusive gold standard) further substantiate these claims of the failure of higher education. Too little higher learning occurs over time in college, as the Wabash and Richard Arum studies cited in Chapter 1 conclude. The American Institutes for Research (AIR) found that 75 percent of two-year college students and 50 percent of four-year college students did not perform at proficient levels of literacy on tasks such as summarizing competing arguments in newspaper editorials or comparing competing credit card offers with differing interest rates.[23] The same study found that 20 percent of college graduates had only basic quantitative skills; for example, they were unable to correctly calculate the total cost of an order of office supplies, figure their way through comparisons of ticket prices, or correctly sum the price of a salad plus a sandwich on a lunch menu. And a 2007 National Center for Education Statistics study found that only 31 percent of college graduates could read a complex book and take away lessons or messages from the text.[24]

Conclusion

We are justifiably concerned about college quality, the primacy of faith-based assessments of the value of an institution's educational programs, the lack of comparative data (or even reliable institutional data) about the quality and quantity of learning, and the distressing ineffectiveness of our colleges and universities. But those concerns must not overwhelm our recognition that certain kinds of important learning do occur in colleges of any type. In *How College Affects Students*, a landmark review of thirty years of research on college learning across all colleges and universities, Ernest Pascarella and Patrick Terenzini reported that simply going to college—any college—positively affects learning. Students leave with improved cognitive skills, greater verbal and quantitative competence, and more highly developed political, social, and religious attitudes and values. This information is at least slightly reassuring. After adjusting for the quality of entering freshmen, though, Pascarella and Terenzini found wide variations in learning within each institution but *not* significant differences between colleges. Moreover, they found that where one attends college contributes less to success than does attaining a bachelor's degree versus a high-school diploma.[25] What would the president or director of admissions speaking to a crowd of prospective students and their parents have to say about that?

If presidents or directors of admissions had gathered good data about learning at their institution, they might talk about true higher learning—about the developmental characteristics of learning in college, about the ways in which research about the neurobiology of learning have begun to transform pedagogy and promote student success, and about the methods of assessing learning directly. We turn to those topics in the three chapters that follow.

3

The Developmental Basis of Higher Learning

Developmental Learning

True *higher* learning, as we defined it earlier—learning that prepares students to think creatively and critically; communicate effectively; and excel in responding to the challenges of life, work, and citizenship—is fundamentally developmental. When learning is developmental, it inspires, reinforces, and reflects the growth and maturation of the learner as a whole human being. Learning that is developmental is not limited to the acquisition of new information; it is centered in the potential for change in the learner as a result of engagement with new knowledge and experiences. It acknowledges challenge and change as essential to growth and maturation. To be transformative, learning must be developmental.[1]

Human development—the observable patterns of growth and maturation at any stage of life—is itself a process of learning. It represents the gradual emergence of a human being who eventually becomes complete, or whole, in relation to the self, others, society, the world, and the universe. Those development processes do not occur as a mere backdrop for the acquisition and application of knowledge; instead, development is interwoven with knowledge acquisition and application throughout life. Both development and knowledge acquisition and application are learning. Were we to seek to preserve the mind versus body dichotomy, so deeply but wrongly entrenched in our culture, we might say that learning about the self or the relationship of the self to others was one kind of learning, and learning about history, economics, or astrophysics is another. But there is little or no reason to believe that different kinds of learning exist. Instead, there are just different subjects about which we learn, and learning about one of those subjects inevitably engages learning about many others. It is not possible to learn the content of a discipline without at the same time exploring the connections between and implications of that content for one's personal history, values, and experiences. A developmental view of the purposes, processes, and desired outcomes of learning recognizes and celebrates this inherent integration of learning about the self and learning about the world. In rejecting the dichotomy of mind versus body, we also reject the common differentiation of student development from academic learning in higher education. This developmental view of and approach to learning are consistent with and thoroughly supported by the conclusions of recent research in the neurophysiology of learning. All learning engages the whole person.

Human development occurs progressively, in what psychologists have labeled phases, or stages; developmental learning in higher education should also occur progressively. The goal of higher learning is to make that process of developmental learning intentional, rather than accidental; to inspire it, rather than allow it to happen passively, serendipitously, or by chance; and to support it, rather than neglect it. Achieving these purposes requires that students and teachers use the raw materials of facts, ideas, theories, perspectives, arguments, hypotheses, beliefs, and values to construct intelligence in a dynamic, engaging, and rigorous process that, at its best, enables students to learn in a customized and progressive, though nonlinear, way. Learning designed and experienced in this way has the characteristics of an apprenticeship; during college, teachers mentor students in moving from apprentice to master. This learning apprenticeship sets the stage for lifelong learning.

But, as argued earlier, higher learning—the developmental, transformative learning described here—is missing today in most American undergraduate education. What passes for higher education today is seldom developmental and even less often transformative. Too many college students are failing to learn in a way that supports the goal of their becoming whole, well-rounded, responsible and accountable human beings. Most colleges and universities do not pay enough attention to the "higher" in learning and therefore are not intentional about supporting it. Do we want college graduates simply to be people who have bought a degree? Do we really want to measure the value of their college education by some amount of content they memorized and then forgot by the time they leave campus? Don't we have something deeper and richer in mind when we talk about higher education? The goals of learning in college are, and must be, far broader than the current model of coming to know new facts, gaining specific academic skills, or developing new competencies. The point is not that knowledge does not matter; it absolutely does. The point is that new knowledge by itself is not sufficient to accomplish the goals and purposes of true higher learning. The desired learning goals of college must embrace not simply the active acquisition of knowledge, but also the active and increasingly expert use of that knowledge in critical thinking, problem solving, and coherent communication, as well as the personal, psychic, emotional, social, and civic learning of the student.

Just putting new information into memory and having it stay there intact long enough to get through an exam can itself be challenging, especially for students who are not motivated, not invested in their college education, or not prepared and ready to learn. In other words, even learning that is not "higher" requires some amount of time and effort and is not necessarily instant and easy. Cramming is an energy-dependent, time- and resource-consuming activity. But assessing the quality of new information, evaluating the trustworthiness of its source, discerning its significance, uncovering the deeper meaning of it, figuring out how it might link to other knowledge already gained, and identifying the need for additional knowledge to help make sense of the new information just acquired are all steps that involve different and much more strenuous—and developmental—learning tasks. Accordingly, higher learning requires not only intellectual mastery by students but also a journey into themselves; only through that journey can each student really make meaning of new knowledge. As would be true of any apprenticeship, this endeavor requires demanding and caring teachers.

Nondevelopmental Learning

There is little attention paid in higher education today to the idea of higher learning as apprenticeship. Instead, most of the current explanatory models of college learning use mechanical or business, rather than developmental, assumptions and metaphors. One particularly invidi-ous idea holds that students' minds traverse educational systems and requirements as if they were pulled along on a conveyor belt in some manufacturing plant; central to that idea is the construct of empty heads being progressively filled up with knowledge (here, content may actually be the appropriate term, unfortunately) as they are processed from class to class and eventually arrive fully assembled, as it were, at graduation. Not very different are equally cynical formulations of college education that liken it to banking. Paulo Freire's sarcastic version of a banking met-aphor suggests that professors deposit knowledge into students' minds through lectures—in which knowledge flows in only one direction, from teacher to student; when asked, students must retrieve that knowledge and offer it back.[2] We might optimistically imagine that a student's "bal-ance" of information gradually increases, but it is impossible not to won-der how such a model of education would account for withdrawals or insufficient funds, never mind stop payment orders and cash advances. A more systemic banking metaphor holds that the college or university itself is a kind of bank of deposited knowledge. Everything the institution knows and the resources it provides to preserve, shape, or disseminate that knowledge are assets: courses, libraries, technology, and professors, presumably. Students enroll in college for the purpose of using those assets, which the institution permits them to do, subject to the regular and timely payment of tuition, for specific periods of time. But the latter metaphor of the college as a bank is perhaps the most alarming on many levels, not the least of which is the implication that the institution has no responsibility for quality of learning and no accountability for helping students use its assets in the most productive ways—just as a financial institution has no responsibility for how its customers use the funds they have withdrawn or deposited there.

These mechanical metaphors reek of standardization and insult both students and educators; do we really think students coming to college are empty-headed, or that teachers should just mumble content and await its successful regurgitation? Learning of the caliber we would define as higher cannot be understood or described with those metaphors. Neither students (whether seen as minds on conveyor belts or depositors of infor-mation bits) nor institutions (understood to be banks of assets) should be as passive or disengaged as such limited conceptions would suggest.

The Integration of Development and Learning in Higher Education

Consider an apocryphal but telling anecdote about a set of parents who take their son out for a celebratory dinner upon his graduation from college. Throughout the meal, the new graduate and his parents engage in a friendly yet passionate debate about the merits and drawbacks of the nation's foreign and domestic policy. At the end of a stimulating and enlightening evening, the son turns to his parents and exclaims, "How on earth did you both learn so much in the four years I was away?"[3] In a quotation commonly attributed to him, Mark Twain recounted his personal version of this story as follows: "When I was a boy of 14, my father was so ignorant I could hardly stand to have the old man around. But when I got to be 21, I was astonished at how much the old man had learned in seven years." Something fundamental has changed during the years that intervened between the student's high school and college graduations—and of course, contrary to the his assertion, the locus of change doesn't lie within the parents.

Fundamental to the concepts of development and learning is the idea of progression: we develop (or construct) new or more complex cognitive, emotional, relational, and social abilities as we grow and mature. This continuous reconstruction of the way we understand the world and ourselves is a natural and lifelong process, occurring in a succession of stages, each of which is literally a transformation from the last. These stages ascend like a staircase, each new step building on prior learning but also enabling a greater capacity to derive meaning that is increasingly complex and more psychologically and emotionally satisfying.

Students at successive stages of development are able to generate, use, and appreciate new perspectives because they become able to use progressively and successively more advanced and mature logic, different and more sophisticated forms of reasoning to draw their conclusions. Their ability to use new and more demanding forms of logic cannot be attributed simply to getting older or having been taught more; it reflects an increasingly complex mechanism of making sense of the world. This is certainly informed by additional knowledge and experience, but it also arises from the development of a qualitatively different kind and form of comprehension over time. As we gradually gain knowledge and greater experience of the physical and social world at any age and are challenged about what we know and how we know it by parents, teachers, friends, and media, we grow in our capacity to understand relationships between ideas; between external objects; among ourselves and our parents, siblings, and friends; among individuals, including ourselves, and the larger community(s) in which we live; and among our own personal, internal identities.

Here is an example. Compare the comprehension of eighth graders, who read *Gulliver's Travels* as a fable about interesting adventures with little people, giants, horses, and flying islands, to that of college seniors, who read the same book as an artful political and social satire about eighteenth-century England and as a profound commentary on human nature, friendship, and the limits of government. The story itself does not change; college students read the same words, but they find different meaning in them. Why? Not only because they have more knowledge and experience, but because they have developed a greater capacity to understand relationships among ideas. They have found new lenses through which they can see things in new ways. Thus both classroom discourse and the famously nocturnal discussions held in residence halls about politics or world affairs gradually become more nuanced as students engage with not only new knowledge and understanding, but also other people—students, professors, resident assistants—whose ideas and allegiances aren't like their own. Most students are forced into—and gradually come to welcome—lively debate.

Crucial in catalyzing and sustaining development is the quantity, quality, and diversity of interactions with others and their ideas. So it is that we constantly construct and restructure what we know through thinking about what we have experienced. This is a continuous and iterative process through which we become cognitively and socially more intelligent as we become developmentally more mature. Children and adolescents who have greater access to spoken language, books, museums, travel, and music and art lessons, for example, develop more extensive vocabularies, greater reading comprehension, and a richer sense of self and others.[4] This helps explain why family socioeconomic status (SES), more than any other variable, predicts students' schooling success[5] (although we hasten to add that the fact that a student's family has a high SES does not guarantee such achievement). Learning environments matter!

We know that development continues during and long after college; it is not surprising then that college learning is advanced and strengthened by exposure to the greatest possible diversity of ideas, people, and learning experiences, inside and outside the classroom. The much-maligned general education programs required of most undergraduates might address this opportunity if they were far more carefully designed, implemented, and assessed; as it is, most general education is disconnected, unchallenging, and boring. Neither students nor institutions invest much in it. No wonder students so often hate it, and no wonder it so seldom achieves its goals.

We now know that this process of development—what we observe as students grow and mature—has a physical, organic basis in brain development. Brain development creates the foundation for a greater capacity for meaning making; like all other kinds of learning, from becoming fluent in another language to interpreting the results of experiments designed to better explain cellular mechanisms in aging, its occurrence provides evidence of changes in the brain. Increasing complexity of thought can only happen as a result of brain development, which, in turn, is stimulated by interactions with environmental stimuli. Ultimately, the iterative process of maturation that eventually results in the emergence of a whole person is the visible manifestation of progressive alterations in the structure (microanatomy and nerve cell networks) and functions of the brain.

Development continues throughout life. It does not stop when we reach some particular chronological age. Students who start or return to college later in their lives have their own developmental hurdles and opportunities, just as undergraduates of traditional age do. There are predictable peaks of developmental activity, challenge, and growth during the traditional undergraduate college years, when students face personal, relational, and social challenges that they must tackle independently for the first time—but there are other developmental milestones associated with every other age in life as well. Students may now be undergraduates at many different ages and all of them—traditional or nontraditional, residential or commuter, working or nonworking, first time in college or returning adults—are at some point on their own developmental pathways, each with new potential for growth associated with higher learning.

If any metaphor works for developmental, transformative higher learning in college, it is the one of apprenticeship, as suggested earlier. Apprentices work with masters to develop their knowledge, skills, and capacities. Over time, they become increasingly able to formulate their own ideas; make their own meaning; challenge themselves; and form a secure, autonomous, and stable identity. Different apprentices will work best with different masters; the outcomes, while consistent thematically from apprentice to apprentice, will vary in their specifics and details. Eventually, apprentices achieve their own distinction in particular areas of their interest and ability. Similarly, students, in a working partnership with teachers and mentors, construct knowledge and individualized meaning over time. There is no conveyor belt; there were no deposits or returns, and at no point did the institution that provides the structure for these apprenticeships seem or feel like a bank. Unlike the metaphor of the conveyor belt, the process of developmental learning has no end; unlike the bank, it will never have insufficient funds. Students and their learning are a work continuously in progress.

Student Engagement in Developmental Learning

The idea of human development as we use it here is rooted in the work of the Swiss-born biologist turned psychologist Jean Piaget,[6] whose research provides the foundation for many of the theories that attempt to explain cognitive development and learning from childhood through the adult years. How is it, he asked, that children develop over time so that problems that at one age seem insurmountable can be solved easily several years later? Put in somewhat loftier terms, he sought to demystify the growth and formation of human intelligence.

Given recent research on learning and the brain, it is important to note that Piaget recognized and articulated what is at the heart of development—the interactions between organisms (such as humans) and the environment (the world around them) that produce change, also known as learning.[7] In those interactions, the developing person adapts through processes of assimilation (in which no fundamental change is required) and accommodation (in which there must be modifications of how we think and feel in response to environmental demands).[8]

Consider this example of change in a student's perspective. An entering freshman who has come to college from a conservative family and social background finds her philosophy challenged. At home, she was surrounded by people whose views were generally similar to those she learned from her family. At college, though—a starkly different environment—she is exposed to a more diverse group of people, some of whose ideas challenge her accustomed way of thinking and acting. She discovers political discussions, convictions, and views, in and out of class, that are more liberal than she is used to, but at times she finds herself persuaded by the cogency of others' reasoning. She finds the appeal of new ideas and ways of thinking both exhilarating and disturbing. She is able to reconcile discrepancies between her social conservatism and these new perspectives by conceding some points while retaining a general allegiance to her conservative philosophy. She has incorporated some liberal views, but she has not fundamentally altered her basic philosophy. She assimilated but did not accommodate.

Her initial solution turns out to be a temporary fix, however. Her social conservatism becomes harder to maintain in the following year, when the campus comes alive with controversy over a student health insurance bill being considered by the state legislature. Petitions circulate in support of both the liberal and conservative positions. Unsure of her own stand on this issue, she engages others in discussion, finding herself first challenged and then persuaded by the logic of the more liberal position. Indeed, while still feeling somewhat perplexed by her change of mind, she is asked by her conservative friends to sign their petition. After agonizing for a day, she refuses to sign, and, in their anger, her former conservative allies label her a liberal. Although initially uncomfortable with this designation, she realizes that her political views have actually changed considerably. Not only does she agree with the liberals on specific issues, but also her overall approach to political and social questions has changed. Now she has accommodated her political philosophy to new environmental conditions and, in that process, her philosophy itself has been reorganized.

Other examples might illustrate assimilation and accommodation in a different direction. A student who transfers from an urban community college initially holds strong views about universal health care and a single payer model but finds that other students in his economics classes make persuasive points about the limitations and costs of those approaches; eventually, as he tracks debates about health care reform, he comes to believe that the benefits of universal health care do not justify the costs. His old friends and family cannot believe that he has dropped his allegiance to a principle they continue to defend, and the student acknowledges that he is rethinking his social and political philosophy.

These stories illustrate an important point: the mind does not simply absorb or bank discrete data that it encounters but seeks to organize those data in some relation to what it already knows—in other words, to construct meaning, and meaning that is idiosyncratic to each individual. Development is that constant evolution of cognitive and emotional intelligence. It represents the human mind's tendency to systematize its processes as coherently as possible and, when necessary, to reorganize those systems in response to changing environmental stimuli. The simple question, "What does that mean to you?" when asked by a teacher as a student ponders a poem, a photograph, a historical narrative, the results of a research study, the structure of an organic compound, or a problem in astrophysics immediately brings the learner into the learning. "What does that mean to you?" at once dismisses both conveyor belts and banks as learning metaphors.

Developmental learning is catalyzed by a tide of environmental stimuli, both inside and outside the classroom, and this fact lies at the heart of how we think about what ought to be taught for developmental learning in higher education. In college, students of any age inevitably meet new challenges that they cannot immediately overcome with their prior knowledge and established ways of understanding. They are intellectually and/or emotionally thrown off balance, as it were, when they lack the tools with which to respond adequately in a new situation. New and different knowledge and explanations in history, literature, science, and mathematics learned in college, for example, compete with what was known previously. Courses in the natural sciences, philosophy, art, or economics raise new perspectives and questions. An introductory biology course might upend a student's confidence in creationism. More in-depth knowledge of economic systems may lead another student to modify her strong views about the government's role in social security or medical care. A professor asks for further explanation of a point a student just made, or a classmate offers a competing point of view, and the student feels at that moment thrown for a loop and left at a momentary loss for words. Processing is required; comparisons of old and new knowledge must be filtered through traditional perspectives, which may or may not survive. This is at the very least uncomfortable; it stretches students. In the instants of debate or challenge, anxiety may trump thought. The brain needs more time and experience to help formulate a new architecture of connections among competing and conflicting ideas and knowledge.

Until those connections—and meanings—are made, any student can feel confused, question what he or she believes, and experience increased feelings of insecurity. This experience can sometimes push individuals to the point of psychological crisis as their fundamental understanding of the world is shattered and must be reconstructed. But living through and getting past such experiences—as we all do—are essential parts of the developmental process.

Here is another example: first-year college students who, having been raised in one particular religious tradition for their entire lives, now discover very different perspectives and beliefs in their courses and in building relationships with new peers. This may at first spark questions about which religion is the "right one" for the first time. If no satisfying answer is forthcoming, as is often the case, students may begin to rephrase the question in deeper and more difficult terms. They might experience the need to examine the role of faith in the midst of uncertainty and truth in human existence. These questions can be genuinely threatening to students' sense of self, their ingrained beliefs, and how they have always functioned in the world. It is not bad that this occurs; it is profoundly important and good that it does. The discomfort—however long it lasts—is worthwhile.

Individuals facing this kind of developmental challenge come to recognize that they must change something to persevere. This requires that they make deep-seated adaptations in their ways of seeing and doing. Generally the new ways of responding they develop are more complex than the old because they have incorporated lessons learned from current environmental challenges and have now become more flexible and capable to handle future challenges. This is an essential step toward psychological, emotional, and intellectual resiliency. Students questioning their faith in college may eventually arrive at a more intricate understanding of spirituality—one that acknowledges different religious expressions by different people in different contexts, but at the same time affirms their own personal decisions about what to believe while allowing room for future challenges and further development. Resilience and persistence are critical in such situations; they do not develop without challenge.

The challenge for higher education is to intentionally spur development by purposefully exposing students to and engaging them in a milieu of new and different ideas, people, and cultures. In and out of the classroom, on and off campus, prefabricated knowledge and unexplored connections between ideas leave many students, particularly those who are struggling with other challenges, fundamentally underdeveloped. The task is not to just keep students busy, but to engage them—by requiring purposeful reflection, research, writing, and speaking and by creating connections, intellectually and emotionally, with peers, professors, and student affairs professionals. Ultimately, our purpose is to couple, or connect, their learning experiences in ways that are both developmentally and intellectually coherent.

The Challenge of Change: Transformative Learning

The idea that higher education will qualitatively change students unnerves or scares some parents (and students); they may fear that learning in college is some process of political or doctrinal brainwashing, that exposure to all those new ideas, different people, and multiple ways of understanding the world might change a son or daughter in negative or unwanted ways. Suppose whatever happens in college "makes my son gay," makes him disrespect his parents, turns him into an atheist! Suppose it turns a daughter against her family's values. Suppose college undermines children's interest in running the family business. What would a parent do then? What if it turns the student into a [fill in the blank] (Republican, Democrat, liberal, conservative)? But learning research tells us that both the process and the fact of intellectual and emotional growth can—and should—at times be unsettling, confusing, and disorienting. Yes, students in the midst of intellectual and personal challenges may miss or misinterpret signs and signals; learning activities designed to open the mind may feel dangerous or threatening, especially when certainty and absolutes are highly valued. This is because challenges to points of view and personal beliefs or attitudes have not just intellectual, but also emotional registers. Like lake effect snow squalls, the debates, challenges, and different perspectives that inspire rethinking of anything from history to personal identity blow in unexpectedly, lower visibility, and disrupt plans.

This is, of course, exactly what one wants; the squall clears, the dust settles, things look different, and a student grows. In the end, students are no worse for the wear; rather, they become heartier, more confident, and more resilient, for they have overcome an obstacle or navigated an experience that may previously have seemed impossible. No endorsement of higher education should suggest that it will be always pleasant and affirming; no college education worth its name should try to be. The politics, mode of dress, and communications style of the suddenly aversive roommate cause discomfort; those experiences stimulate adaptive responses that create a foundation for managing conflict and coping with stress later in life. Yes, that conservative or Marxist speaker said unsettling things, and yes, the range of religious beliefs among others on campus contradicts any viable sense of absolutes.

Everything about higher learning is about openness to the world, the innumerable ideas and values held by others, and the exploration of many options, all in the service of making better sense of the world and our place in it. The point is to find one's own truth—to expand, build, and grow; to make one's own meaning of the complex welter of facts, figures, and narratives that tell the story of human life and purpose; to weigh as many points of view as necessary before determining one's own perspective; to find, test, and experience one's unique identity as a person in relation to oneself, others, society, and the world—and, then, in the end, to put it all together—to compose life, identity, and meaning for oneself. This is the educational purpose of the need to engage diversity of people, ideas, and experiences in college. That process, and its outcomes, will be different for each student. The ambiguity of its pathways and destinations does not make higher education dangerous; the fact that students each make their own meaning of certain elements of knowledge does not disturb the integrity of the knowledge itself.

It is neither indoctrination nor allegiance to any specific set of ideas or systems of thought that we should expect of college; on the contrary, the idea of higher education is centered in liberation—in introducing students to the extraordinary freedom of the human mind. Higher education, when practiced in ways that do justice to its heritage and ideals, counters indoctrination. In the end, some students will tough their way through any number of intellectual and developmental snow squalls without seriously or meaningfully inquiring into the assumptions and beliefs that came with them to college. We might say their college or university education has failed them. But when higher learning works, students ought to change significantly, and for the better.

To say that the process of higher learning finds its own pathway in each student, and that its specific results will be different for every student, is not to say that it does not have certain desirable outcomes across the diversity of students and colleges. To say that it is an idiosyncratic and mysterious process does not mean that its outcomes are vague or impractical. The capacity to analyze and evaluate ideas and opinions—one of those desired outcomes—is different from allegiance to any particular idea. The ability to understand oneself but also to take the perspective of another is essential to any graduate's success in today's diverse, global economy—and it is different from endorsing a specific political perspective or proselytizing a belief system. Being able to work with others, to function effectively as a member of team, and to be ethical and accountable for the quality of one's work are characteristics desired in families, workplaces, organizations, and civic endeavors. Higher education, therefore, is preparation for life in a global society.

Herein lies the critical opportunity for faculty members to intentionally promote developmental growth in their classrooms. Each and every discipline encompasses and imparts not only facts, but the tools for understanding and integrating those facts—concepts, paradigms, principles, and language, for example, that help students relate new information to what came before it, as well as comprehend how to apply that information in new situations. But only if students are expected to practice such learning will it happen. Imagine the initial response of students, for example, who have successfully memorized math formulas to answer high school test questions, being asked for the first time in college to explain how they arrived at the answer. Or students who are confronted with courses in history, literature, sociology, psychology, religion, or anthropology that challenge their attitudes about gender, race, and sexual orientation. The mastery of new facts and tools of inquiry helps students develop increasing capacities to think critically, appreciate different perspectives, and solve problems. With such learning they are better equipped and more secure in their own identity, autonomy, and connection to others. Dishing out more content is not the means to achieving these ends. Rather, we must ask students to confront and manage the uncertainty and disequilibrium they feel when they are engaged in learning experiences for the purpose of increasing knowledge and comprehension, improving resiliency, and resolving conflict. As students engage with new ideas and emotions, they develop. To do so they need dialectical and challenging pedagogy and curriculum that foster diverse and competing perspectives. This is what fuels a level of engagement that results in higher learning.

Such learning requires a far greater investment of time, focus, and intensity of effort, by both the teacher and the learner. Here, then, is an inescapable fact: higher learning is not only qualitatively different but requires harder work by everyone. Professors who elevate expectations for the quality and quantity of student effort must simultaneously commit to a greater quality and quantity of effort from themselves as well. Writing-intensive assignments and courses, regularly assessing the quality of students' work and giving frequent feedback, for example, are more rigorous and demanding for professors than recycling multiple choice exams and assigning grades based purely on the percentage of correct answers.

Developmental teaching and learning require greater investments, more work, and more time precisely because developmental approaches acknowledge the fundamental reality of higher learning: that students learn more about themselves and the world at the same time; that their growth as persons parallels the increase in their knowledge, intellectual sophistication, and mental capacities. It is not possible to imagine true higher learning absent the journey into the self; making meaning demands the participation of the whole person, encumbered or elevated as he or she may be by life and its welter of events and experiences. Take the student as a person out of the learning and you are back to the bank—or, worse, the conveyor belt. Understood in this way, higher education requires far more from students than reproducing assigned information, completing a prescribed number of courses or credit hours, or donning a cap and gown at graduation; it requires the expanding of the cognitive and emotional capacity for imagination, the ability to think critically and solve problems, and the facility to judge what is relevant, accurate, and moral. A college education that omits these necessary elements of the student's development and maturation does not provide higher learning.

Implications for Higher Learning

Higher learning is existentially challenging because the essential stimulus for developmental growth is the conflict created by purposeful interactions with different ideas, perspectives, and people. Encountering both extraordinary diversity and novel independence, college students of any age—not just the historically typical eighteen- to twenty-four-year-old undergraduate—must make sense of numerous and often unfamiliar or conflicting perspectives. Moreover, this new process of learning becomes a deeply personal endeavor, as students question what they believe, why they believe it, and even who they are. Profound questions about the meaning of life and the nature of the human condition that may have incubated during high school are now pushed to the foreground for first-time undergraduates; the fundamental uncertainties facing students who come to college after having other life experiences differ, but are similarly highlighted by beginning, or returning to, college. Both brain development and human development continue long after the traditional undergraduate years; students who are much older than twenty can learn and change when they engage with higher education; there is no time limit on transformation. The formation of a more flexible and complex ability to think, the exploration of identity, the cultivation of relationships, and the cementing of an ethical grounding ought to be deeply influenced by the myriad disciplines of knowledge and innumerable learning experiences students explore.

The distinct and unparalleled flood of challenges that colleges supply to undergraduates makes the experience, at its best, supremely developmental. Classically, traditional age undergraduates are newly exposed to a wide range and many types of diversity—ideas, people, experiences—that they often experience as overwhelming. Even students who think they have seen this diversity in the media or experienced it through social networking have rarely been so directly involved with it, live and in person, before college. This condition is—or should be—created intentionally through the curricula, pedagogy, and out-of-classroom learning experiences offered by institutions of higher education. At the same time, students are at a distance or removed from the traditional authority figures—parents, teachers, and clergy, for example—upon whom they previously relied for explanation and interpretation of the world. To various degrees, those conditions also apply to undergraduates who are returning adult learners; it is a serious mistake to assume that students who are older than, or have more life experience than, traditional age undergraduates do not face developmental challenges in the college environment. Think of college as an existential crucible, and development as both the source of the fire within the crucible and as the changes that it produces. How better to explore identity, examine and sort out different perspectives, test one's own ideas, and understand one's place in the world than to spend four or five years in college, whether those years occur immediately after high school or later?

Extensive scholarly literature describes the extraordinarily rich developmental moment that college can, and should, represent.[9] High school graduates largely see the world in terms of black-and-white absolutes; the same may be true of some older students coming to college for the first time. This is not to their discredit; it is a consequence of developmental stage and capacity. But the uncertainty and confusion sparked by interactions with new ideas and people in college inevitably lead to the realization that there are many gray areas in the realms of knowledge and truth. Students may turn to new experts, advisors, or mentors for help in sorting through the depths of those gray areas, but once they recognize that professors and advisors, counselors, and administrators at college don't have all the answers, the search turns inward. Students start to recognize their own selves as legitimate sources of knowledge and authority. This newfound trust of self may produce a tentative kind of independence that inspires the portrayal of the awkwardly amusing but frustrating college kid caricatured in so many television shows and movies. More seriously, that tentativeness—which is a developmental reality—explains why colleges seek to balance educational and punitive approaches in managing students' behavioral aberrations when their offenses cause no danger to self or others. Minor violations of campus codes of student conduct, for example, generate requirements for written essays about the impact of the student's action on others, rather than onerous fines or expulsions. Learning to accept responsibility for one's actions is a legitimate goal of developmental learning—which is why addressing issues of plagiarism, behavior related to alcohol and other drug abuse, and obtaining consent for sexual activities are such salient college issues.

As they move through college, students are repeatedly confronted with complex, high-stakes issues that create deep divides among those around them. Exposure to their passionate (and sometimes wrong, but never in doubt) peers, the divergent convictions of professors, and the increasingly intricate but also potentially contradictory lessons of different disciplines helps students learn to acknowledge legitimate expertise, recognize the importance of context, understand the relative validity of some arguments over others, and appreciate the need to present evidence for their own beliefs. These key transformations may seem to be primarily cognitive in nature, but students are also maturing emotionally, learning appropriate, practiced, and mature ways of managing feelings.[10] Now removed from the familiar and highly structured support systems at home, students of traditional undergraduate age must learn how to balance their newfound sense of independence while increasing their resourcefulness and ability to ask for help when they need it. These are critical elements to establishing identity—a key developmental task for students—as any parent whose child returns home after the first year of college with a different hair color, new piercing, startling political affiliation, or unexpected significant other will attest. Other questions of identity, purpose, and relationships arise for returning adult learners and other nontraditional undergraduates. Students are works in progress at any age; as they develop the capacity for self-reflection, they envision who they are becoming and who they want to become as individuals and work toward integrating the multiple facets of self, including gender, race, ethnicity, spirituality, and sexuality, into a coherent whole.

Students' interpersonal relationships undergo significant change and growth during this formative time as well.[11] Students face the obvious challenge of having to establish new peer networks at college, and they are simultaneously forced to relate to others from very different backgrounds. They must learn how to build some degree of harmony within a new community, which typically involves learning how to resolve conflict through communication, negotiation, and compromise. The experience of having a roommate is often in and of itself both new and profoundly developmental for students who live on campus; considering another person's preferences in matters as mundane as who gets which bed or as complicated as respecting different religious beliefs and practices enables a student to begin learning how to take the perspective of another. Students must learn how to both tolerate and appreciate differences in others and how to handle diversity positively and constructively. Besides all the new people students will meet, they find a plethora of social outlets on display and ready for exploration—clubs and activities, student government, various interest groups, intercollegiate and intramural sports, fraternities and sororities, and volunteer service projects. Participation in those groups and experiences helps students learn in practical and applied ways that strengthen their ability to make meaning of what they are studying in courses or other formal academic programs. For example, reading about organizations and leadership produces only abstract knowledge, but joining and seeking office in a student organization grounds it.

The development process that is catalyzed by the many diverse elements inherent in the college experience involves more than just intellectual growth. Emotion plays a vital role in motivating the use of intellect. The reverse is true as well: cognition precipitates affect. Something in the environment catches our attention—a beautiful painting, for example—and we react with feeling ("It moved me to tears"). Something in the environment spurs our interest—the bright colors and movement of a mobile above the crib, a cat purring, a line of poetry, a melodic sound, the power of a sermon, the point well made in a professor's lecture—and we pause and inquire. We are moved to explore something within ourselves as a result of a sense of puzzlement or contradiction—a teacher's question, the frowning gesture of a friend, an injustice witnessed. We know that a person who is emotionally cut off cannot function well cognitively; reciprocally, a person unable to cognitively control his or her emotions cannot function interpersonally.

We attribute meaning to emotions through our cognitive capacity, and as we develop intellectually, we also increase our capacity for more complex and meaningful emotional understanding—leading, for example, to a more adequate capacity for perspective taking. The capacity for perspective taking—the ability to accurately apprehend and reflect another's thinking, emotions, and motivation in a given situation—is an integral developmental outcome of college education central to the formation of social and moral competence and capacity for intimacy. Embedded in this notion is the perceiver's capacity for empathy, without which taking someone else's perspective would represent nothing more than an emotionally detached cognitive exercise (akin to one's hearing a group of people who were victimized by extreme discrimination and merely responding with "Yes, I see your point"). Perspective acting is an individual's competence in translating his or her understanding of another's viewpoint into actions—the capacity to use the information gathered in perspective taking to act in a normatively reasonable and justifiable way. These abilities develop over time, requiring contact with different, challenging, and diverse ideas and people that serve as the fuel for development.

Development also involves increasing capacity for intimacy marked by the formation of healthy relationships—relationships that are characterized by stability, interdependence, equality, and mutuality. The stakes around this developmental challenge are high; students' safety and wellness are the result of such positive interactions early on in their college years. But this aspect of development is also critical because it sets the stage for the way students will relate to others throughout their lives—whether they can balance trusting others with maintaining boundaries, whether they can meet the fundamental human need for intimacy and attachment, and, ultimately, whether they can live at peace with others in their world. As students struggle to belong in the campus community, they come face to face with the realization that community membership is not granted simply because one is physically present; rather, it involves understanding social norms and rules, behaving in ways that are congruent with and support community expectations, and balancing one's individual needs with those of others. These are the building blocks of the development of a well-rounded, solidly grounded adult.

Developmental Challenges Today

The plethora of developmental tasks and hurdles that awaits college students requires a degree of readiness or capacity on the part of the student. Students who have significant psychological challenges may respond less well than their peers to the essential and existential questions that higher learning inevitably entails. The majority of students come to college reasonably prepared to confront those issues. But larger numbers and percentages of students are coming to college with significant psychological burdens.[12] More than ten years ago, Arthur Levine and Jeanette Cureton provided a veritable menu of students' psychological and behavioral problems, including increases over the previous two decades in the prevalence of eating disorders (by 58 percent), classroom disruption (by 44 percent), drug abuse (by 42 percent), gambling (by 25 percent), and suicide attempts (by 23 percent).[13] They reported that 51 percent of sexually active students admitted not practicing safer sex, and they, like other observers, described dramatic increases in the use of counseling and psychological services provided by colleges.[14] The authors described in stark terms the overall impact of these behavioral issues on both the individual student and the campus community:

> The effect of the accumulated fears and hurts that students have experienced is to divide and isolate them. Undergraduates have developed a lifeboat mentality of sorts. It is as if each student is alone in a boat in a terrible storm, far from any harbor. The boat is taking on water and believed to be in imminent danger of sinking. Under these circumstances, there is but one alternative: each student must single-mindedly bail. Conditions are so bad that no one has time to care for others who may also be foundering. No distractions are permitted. The pressure is enormous and unremitting.[15]

Since the publication of their work in 1998, concerns about the readiness, resilience, and psychological well-being of traditional age undergraduates have become commonplace in both public and professional literature. Newspapers and professional journals regularly publish articles about the challenges counseling centers face in providing sufficient services. There are many reasons for the apparent increase in mental health problems among students, however. The earlier recognition and treatment of mental health problems, the easier availability and far greater social acceptability of both psychotherapy and psychotropic medications, changes in both formal and informal institutional policies and practices regarding the admission of or assistance to students with histories of mental health problems, aggressive enrollment competition, changes in patterns of childrearing (including the phenomenon of the helicopter parent), and rising expectations of parents are all factors, as may be a true increase in the prevalence of some mental health problems, such as depression. Although there is no such thing as an acceptable rate of suicide among students, there is also no sound evidence that the rates of suicide in college students or their same-age peers who are not in college have increased in recent years.

The challenge in higher education is to respond sufficiently to the serious, more intense needs of some students without failing to promote the healthy development of the larger community of students. Colleges and universities are neither social service agencies nor mental health centers; society cannot reasonably expect that institutions of higher education will provide ongoing, long-term care for students whose psychological challenges undermine their own learning—or interfere with the learning and educational experience of other students. Institutions must seek to balance the allocation of scarce mental health resources among students who require in-depth clinical services; students who have traditional, lower-intensity psychological concerns; and students, most of whom do not seek individual services, who would benefit from outreach programs and interventions that improve the learning environment.

One can acknowledge statistical changes in the frequencies of certain behaviors and the prevalence of some dysfunctional conditions without losing hope, but such data do suggest that college is not necessarily "the best years of your life" for every student. It is important to remember that most undergraduates—of any age and previous life experience, regardless of the personal and psychological challenges they may face—seem more resilient than defeated, more flourishing than foundering. But students, while appearing to be quite together, may use dysfunctional workarounds to manage the enormous and unremitting pressure that Levine and Cureton describe (for instance, "work hard, play hard" and its alcohol-related consequences).

Barriers to Integrative, Developmental Learning

Too many students in college do not have the opportunity for, or are failing at, the developmental learning that is central to their progress toward the goal of becoming whole, well-rounded, responsible human beings. Colleges and universities do not sufficiently catalyze holistic developmental learning (at any age, and for any category of learners) in intentional ways.

Too often, they inspire only the intellectual, or cognitive, dimension of overall learning. This happens primarily because many faculty members still think of learning as one thing and development as another; they do not yet embrace a comprehensive view of developmental learning that allies, rather than distinguishes and separates, the two. Terminology does not help in this regard. While the idea of human development rightly incorporates cognitive or intellectual development as well as emotional, psychological, and social development, the term student development in practice has come to mean nonacademic experiences provided typically by student affairs professionals, who are usually also expected to deliver certain consumer services and enforce the code of conduct while keeping students happy and satisfied, rather than the faculty. Learning, on the other hand, has been located exclusively in the intellect and in the classroom. Learning experiences outside the classroom—especially if they are also outside the traditional academic curriculum—are judged as inferior and unworthy of serious attention—and certainly not considered valid or valuable enough to warrant academic credit. The false separation of a narrow sense of academic and other learning (inside and outside the classroom, respectively) reinforces the dichotomy of mind versus body, and of intellect versus person, that prevails in higher education.

Keeping the noncognitive, nonintellectual components of developmental learning out of the curriculum and classroom has become both possible and normative because of the differences in the ways in which faculty members and student affairs professionals are prepared, in the structuring of the work they do, and the kinds of education they provide. It would be unfair and wrong to say that faculty members do not care about students, or are indifferent to their personal, social, and emotional challenges and needs. But, often unwittingly, they perpetuate this focus on cognition; generally, they do not receive formal training in teaching and/or learning and have little specific knowledge of their students' developmental needs or how they can support them. In their minds, there is a load of content to cover and not enough time to get everything in. Thus at a stage when students need mentors and role models for intellectual and developmental growth, faculty members are focused principally on students' absorption of knowledge.

The organization and administration of the institution parallels these distinctions: academic affairs deals with the intellect and the mind, and student affairs deals with the body, psyche, emotions, and spirit. It takes little observation to tell which of the two has greater value in higher education. Unquestionably, academic learning in the narrow and flat intellectual sense is treated as far superior and of greater relevance to the purpose and mission of colleges and universities. But the point is not the relative power or imputed value of the "two sides of the house," as they are called; learners and learning are integrated wholes, and they inhabit both sides of the house at the same time. So learning, as a holistic process that should engage students in a fully developmental way, is fractured on our campuses; faculty and student affairs staff are relegated to independent territories divided not by bad intentions, but by traditions, tensions, and training. Paradoxically, this well-established pattern of practice in higher education actually undermines not only learning experiences outside the classroom, but also the quality of curricular, classroom-based learning as well. This divide costs our students greatly. Brains do not stop developing (which means learning) when students leave the classroom. Students don't learn in compartmentalized ways; they learn continuously, always and everywhere, and the organization of learning—or, from the institution's perspective, teaching—overlooks that simple fact.

Academic learning—what we have earlier called the acquisition and application of knowledge—does not alone sufficiently advance personal, emotional, social, and civic maturation, much less foster integration and coherence in learning. Intellectual growth, among too many faculty members, is understood as sufficient accretion of knowledge rather than as far more complex and integrative in nature. Without a developmental consciousness and approach, academic learning comes regrettably close to what is imagined in the mechanical metaphors described earlier. Inherent in the current academic learning model is the neat, simple, and discrete packaging of information—content—that students can file away in the proper places. Absent meaning making, information does indeed become just content—abstracted knowledge without personal significance or grounding for any student. The poem is the poem, the fact is the fact, the equation is the equation; it is all just data, or content. Knowledge is thus divided up into territories—academic disciplines, each with its specific courses—and students are left to connect the dots among those courses and disciplines for themselves, if they can. The institution neither assumes nor makes those connections, and it does not often look to see if they were made; the sequence of courses in a major may give students depth in the discipline, but it imparts no breadth in the larger questions of human life and experience. In other words, there are rarely any formalized mechanisms—whether specific courses, reflective seminars, inquiry groups, or learning assessments—to help students integrate their learning or consolidate their accounts, if you will. Indeed, faculty members who lack training in learning naively believe it is fully up to the student to weave together the myriad data variously presented within and across courses, not realizing that learning how to create such integration requires the faculty to also provide expectations, standards, modeling, support, and timely feedback for such meaning making. Knowledge that is purely content-based rapidly seems irrelevant to students, with no pertinence to their lives—so why would they invest in (i.e., put time and effort into) learning?

While the banking metaphor admittedly oversimplifies conditions in higher education, its close approximation in practice is the ubiquitous, often stultifying, passive experience of purely lecture-based teaching. Spend five minutes in most crowded lecture halls and assess the levels of engagement with the material that students exhibit. Rustling newspapers, stifled yawns, frequent text messaging, and covert attention to email messages and websites are far more common than sustained engagement with the lecturer and the topic. Function follows form; students retain little of the information—once again, content works here—and have an inadequate understanding of the meaning of the material beyond its importance in passing exams. Faculty members expect little from students ("Just say enough in the paper and get enough right on the exam to prove that I wasn't completely wasting my time with you") and little is given in return ("What do I have to know to pass the test?"). This is not to say that lectures are inherently ineffective, nor that the need to acquire information is unimportant. It is to say that alone, and in their most commonly practiced forms, these are not developmental in orientation and are insufficient as higher learning.

Furthermore, whatever attention is paid to the components of development that are not primarily cognitive and intellectual often assumes a unitary formulation that blends ages and points in life for all students. That first-time-in-college students at age 18 have different developmental needs from returning adult learners or veterans of military service entering college as freshmen, for example, is not routinely considered. Contemporary student development theory has not fully caught up with the diversification of higher education (college students are not all of traditional age, and all are not white, male, heterosexual, privileged, Christian or Jewish, and the products of two-parent families). As a result, students of any age and previous experience are, in too many institutions, left largely on their own (and in the hands of their peers) to handle developmental challenges.

But integrated developmental learning requires the purposeful linking of what is taught in courses, how that material is taught, and how it might be applied to students' lives outside the classroom—and outside the academy. Whether and to what degree developmental learning—crucial for higher learning—occurs is therefore too often left to chance. In a remarkable and important monograph published by Boston College, *The Journey into Adulthood*, the authors, a diverse group of professors, student affairs professionals, and campus ministers, discussed this reality: "College is a critical stage in the development of young adults. They leave behind old ways of understanding, believing, and relating to the people around them, and move toward new forms of identity and more critically aware forms of knowing, choosing, and living authentically. American colleges and universities have largely moved away from the goal of helping students address the full scope of these challenges, focusing primarily on their intellectual development. The result is a disconnect between the classroom and other parts of students' lives."[16]

Conclusion

The lack of good integration of the academic and out-of-classroom elements of college—and of the intellectual and social, emotional, physical, and spiritual dimensions of students—is, we believe, costly. It means that teaching, understood as transferring knowledge, takes precedence over any more cohesive and coherent approach to learning. It means that colleges do not regularly use the acquisition and exploration of knowledge to catalyze holistic student development. It means colleges are not sufficiently challenging students' perspectives and strengthening their creativity. It undermines real, rigorous learning and obstructs the achievement of desired learning goals. It leaves higher education too mechanistic, linear, and abstracted from students' lives to permit higher learning to occur. It makes college seem incidental, rather than purposeful, in students' minds. It lays a foundation for the graduation of smart students who lose track of vital personal and ethical principles that were inadequately developed during college. It means that society can no longer assume that a college graduate will be broadly educated, trustworthy, and ready for a life of learning and civic and global engagement. And it means that college will seem so irrelevant to students that many will drop out or just make it through.

The pedagogy of developmental learning is significantly different from current practice on most campuses. The levels and types of engagement it requires are the exception, and until they become the rule we will continue to risk losing our minds. The effect of these realities on student outcomes is discouraging. Graduation rates on most college campuses are abysmal: it is not uncommon for colleges to lose more than half of the freshman class by their senior year. This is not a new problem. But rather than losing students (and their minds) because of the rigor of the teaching and curriculum, today's students are more likely to drop out for other reasons—because they are intellectually unprepared, and/or have not been adequately challenged, and, not having had the opportunity to make the critical connections between what they are learning and their own lives, have not mastered the developmental challenges that true higher learning could have helped them overcome. We must put developmental learning back into higher education. Colleges and universities must include the whole range of development as part of their intentional educational purpose. Otherwise students are being shortchanged—at any level of tuition.

4

The Neuroscience of Learning

Introduction

Higher learning changes us. We broaden our understanding of the human and natural worlds, meet people who leave lasting impressions, get to know others who are different from us, and have experiences that make us more capable, teach us important lessons, and inspire us to keep learning. We now know that *higher learning*—at any age—changes our brains as well. In fact, that is what learning is—a process of change in the microscopic structure and functioning of our brains.[1] Neuroscience research shows that learning is a physical, biological, energy-dependent activity (hence the use of the term neurobiological in reference to learning) that occurs in response to sensory inputs—the stimuli that come from our environment. Those stimuli, in all their variety, instigate changes in the connections of neurons to one another (synapses) and in the ways neural networks (the interconnections of many neurons through many synapses) work. Acquiring new knowledge or skills, developing cognitive abilities such as critical thinking, adopting a different perspective or point of view, and becoming expert in any endeavor, from fluency in a second or third language to virtuosity in playing a musical instrument, are examples of the outward and visible manifestations of these basic neurobiological processes and events.[2] We learn when—and because of, and only if—interactions between our brains and the environment (what we call our experiences) cause changes in our brains. We witness those changes when a learner—which means a person of any age who is interacting with his or her environment—demonstrates some new cognitive or other capacity, perspective, or behavior.

Higher learning is then transformational in more than one way. Changing one's mind occurs through changes that happen in one's brain; it means that the intellectual growth and personal and social development that occur in college are based on changes in students' brains as well. In other words, the huge variety of inputs that stimulate learning, from reading to watching a performance to doing a scientific experiment, induce activity in interconnected regions of the brain, and that activity can, if sufficiently powerful and sustained, lead to changes in the structure or function of brain tissue. Such changes are then manifest in students through observable differences in their demonstrated knowledge, attitudes, skills, or behaviors. Instances of learning, aggregated and integrated and extended over time, are the foundation for the gradual, progressive emergence of each distinctive human person—the process of growth and maturation across multiple dimensions that we call human development. The successive phases and stages of human development, which represent the accumulation of changes resulting from many interactions between persons and the world around them, are in fact generated by multitudes of changes in the cells, circuits, and networks of the brain.

The key point is that learning is ultimately a result of the interaction of the brain and the environment. While some basic templates for the core fundamentals of human capacity are hardwired, those templates do not suffice for the full development of a human being. The ability to walk, for example, is based in the genetically determined structures and functions of our brains. But developing those capacities nonetheless requires practice, which means repetitive interactions with the environment—we do, after all, have to learn to walk. Cognitive competency in reading, using language, and doing arithmetic similarly requires many engagements with formal and informal learning experiences. Those multiple interactions, which may include the kinds of repeated, intentional experiences that we call practice, in turn cause increasingly precise and streamlined neurobiological events—changes in the brain that support the achievement of competency and, given sufficient time and intensity of effort, expertise.

From a neurobiological perspective, expertise is efficiency; being an expert at something means that one's brain has adapted—both structurally and functionally—to allow that thing to be done with higher levels of efficiency.[3] The more efficient the brain is at a task—say, playing the violin—the more expert will be the performance of that task, and the more expert the performance, the more efficient the brain. Toddlers become, eventually, experts at walking; changes in some of the nerve cell networks in their brains support (in fact, allow) that process. Depending on our genes, families, interests, cultures, and opportunities, we may also become expert at a few or many other things during our lives. In each case, those competencies arise through the same repetitive cycles of interaction between the brain and some aspect of the environment, whether it is a violin or a set of mathematical formulas. Competency is always both the outcome and the evidence of alterations in the microscopic anatomy and functioning of brain tissue.

The Oneness of Mind and Brain

The separation of mind and body is a central idea in much of Western philosophy, and it has become the basis for many of the policies and organizational models of education. This idea may be for some a reassuring existential construction or a pleasant and relatively low-risk form of self-aggrandizement that helps us feel justified in claiming some superiority over other creatures or distancing ourselves from the relentlessly corporal facts of human life. Regardless, it is complete fiction. The emergence of consciousness and mind in human beings occurred because of, and could not have occurred without, the evolution of the physical organ we call the brain. It is not that the brain is the mind incarnate; rather, the mind—and, therefore, learning—are complex activities of the working brain. *Cogito, ergo sum* ("I think, therefore I am") may capture something about the meaning we may wish to ascribe to our humanity, but it reverses the real order of things: I am, therefore I think.

The tools of the neurosciences and the data collected using those tools have dispelled any serious consideration of the notion that mind is somehow independent of brain and have demonstrated that all information gets into the brain through one or more of the senses. The mind, in other words, has been shown to be not some otherworldly cloud of pure thought floating somewhere in or above the physical being of a person; any vision of the mind as a rarefied entity too glorious and abstract for flesh and blood is a mirage. Elegant experiments clearly locate phenomena such as dreaming, intuition, and creativity in the activity of complex neural networks. Consciousness itself, and our own concepts of self, are properties of the working, physical brain.[4] The distinctive essence of any particular human being arises from the complexity of integrated, unique, and nuanced representations of the world in his or her brain and the distinguishing behaviors and expressions generated from the connections made among those representations—not from some other undefinable quality or force.

There is no mind without brain. Similarly, the relationship between mind and brain is not just a matter of parallel concepts, one of which somehow correlates with the other; the experiences of consciousness and mind are physical and organic expressions of the work of a living, biological organ that consumes resources (oxygen and glucose) and is dependent for those resources on the body that contains it. Breathing, the beating of our hearts, locomotion, singing, and smiling are also physical, energy-dependent activities; they, like learning, are bodily (biological) processes.

Recognizing the oneness of mind and brain—and therefore of mind and body—should rightfully cause us to reassess a great many structures, policies, and practices in education; why, for example, as we pointed out in Chapter 3, do we have those two well-known "sides of the house" in American higher education—academic affairs (mind) and student affairs (body, emotions, spirit)—in separate domains? Do we really think students check their minds at the door when they enter residence halls or leave their bodies behind when they go to class? That they learn only from the formal academic curriculum? That learning happens only during classroom hours?

For perspective: the mind is not made less marvelous by locating it where it actually is, in the brain. Knowing that certain networks of brain cells and particular patterns of the electrical and chemical activity of those cells in communication with other networked cells compose what we call consciousness, memory, thinking, and learning does not denigrate the power or importance of those things. Saying that the mind is a living thing does not undermine its value; indeed, it makes the idea of the life of the mind far more real. And recognizing the mind as a living thing makes our actual experience of life more coherent. We know, for example, that certain disorders of the brain, such as Alzheimer's disease, shrink the mind and reduce the capacity for learning as they destroy the brain. If the mind were not in and of the brain, would that happen? Romantic misconceptions to the contrary notwithstanding, thinking and learning stop when the brain stops.

The Neurobiology of Learning and Development

Every element of learning plays out, anatomically and physiologically, in the brain. It is not sufficient to say that inputs to learning (sensory data, such as hearing, seeing, and feeling), the processes of cognition that respond to those data (various kinds of thinking, such as analysis and problem solving), or the outputs of learning (e.g., formulating expressions of thoughts in speech or writing) are correlated somehow with brain function. More accurately, the inputs, processes, and outputs of learning *are* brain functions. We can see those functions represented with increasing accuracy and inspirational detail in an array of brain imaging technologies. With ever-greater resolution and in both static and moving forms, the images produced by these technologies allow us to witness in new and powerful ways how the brain learns. Our capacity to do so increases—not lessens—our sense of wonder at the extraordinary process that learning is.

Learning can increasingly be visualized, located, and measured through brain imaging techniques that depend methodologically on the relentlessly biological, physical nature of perception, memory, and learning.[5] As with all bodily activity, these critical brain processes are accomplished through work that requires energy, provided by glucose (sugar) and oxygen delivered in the blood, to fuel their activity.[6] It is the delivery of those fuels that make modern functional neuroimaging possible and successful because the methods used in modern imaging measure the levels of those fuels in brain tissue. In other words, the techniques used to watch the brain in action are themselves dependent on the very fact that perception, learning, thinking, and memory are energy-dependent processes of work done by the brain. Were learning not brain based, these tools would not work; they would have no explanatory power.

These imaging techniques reveal conditions in the brain when a person is at rest,[7] perceives sounds,[8] learns to read,[9] experiences emotion,[10] or suffers from one or more pathological conditions in the brain. We can see what part of the brain is stimulated into activity with sensory inputs (such as hearing words or music), processing those inputs, formulating a response (such as thinking of something to say), and generating that response (such as speaking or writing). These techniques can further demonstrate that the brain links old and new representations, or memories, that it has created whenever new information is integrated; reconfigures memories in the process of remembering them; connects emotions to memories and newly received information; and constructs knowledge, or what we might consider to be the products of learning, across neural networks connecting distinct and sometimes remote areas of the brain.[11]

The brain functions holistically, simultaneously combining thinking, feeling, and acting. There is a strong neurophysiological framework for the emotionality with which we may greet challenging new information, pursue new knowledge that promises to bring us desirable rewards, or face changes in our beliefs, perspectives, and understandings of ourselves and the world. Moving images of brain processes show how quickly— and how diffusely—connections among areas of the brain that are specialized for sensing, emotion, thinking, and remembering are made, even in response to simple stimuli; perceiving a single word, for example, is never, at the neurobiological level, just a straightforward matter of receiving auditory sensations that produce a recognizable representation that the brain then interprets as being a certain word.[12] Instead, a complex process occurs with each stimulus: a word is heard, and the sensory data are transformed into signals that reach the brain—after which a variety of areas of brain (including many that are not responsible primarily for hearing itself) process the information transmitted by the word, search for previous associations or memories related to the word, and identify any emotions associated with the word. In the process, the brain distinguishes, for example, "fire" from "Fire!!!!"

Brain imaging reinforces the principle that we are educating the whole student, not just the mind, or intellect—that is, that learning happens in the wholeness of a real person in real time. Watching the display of functional images of the brain at work reminds us that students' minds cannot be separated from their physical, emotional, and social selves; that students come to college whole, learn whole, and should graduate whole. Our attempts to segregate minds from bodies—reinforced by the structures and hierarchies of our campuses—are baseless when viewed in the light of the conclusions of neurophysiological research on learning.

The conclusions of multitudes of neuroscientific studies are the basis for the emerging field of Mind, Brain, and Education, which has generated innovative academic programs and interdisciplinary scholarly journals while spawning meaningful attempts to improve teaching and learning, especially in the K–12 grades. At the same time, the "brain-based learning" movement has produced both well-intentioned proposals for improving childhood learning and ridiculous commercial enterprises that promise hopeful parents and teachers extraordinary results from the adoption of unproven and sometimes silly products alleged to make children smarter.[13]

But the key point underlying both the useful and the awful of those innovations—which is that learning, in fact, occurs in the brain—is absolutely correct; learning is a neurobiological process. We can no longer think seriously of studying learning without studying the brain—and, thus, without addressing also the body in which that brain is contained.[14] Learners, as whole people in whom the brain resides, matter in learning.

Learning as Meaning Making

Learning is a process of meaning making. Each learner acquires and makes meaning of knowledge through a succession of learning experiences; no two learners will understand any material in exactly the same way. What Chicago, or the French Revolution, or a water lily, or the phases of the moon mean to one person will be quite different from what is true for another. That does not mean that Chicago or the water lily as real things change; it means that anyone's knowledge and understanding of Chicago or the water lily is created by his or her own unique history of experiences in relation to gathering and synthesizing information about those things. Every encounter with new information about them generates some new or readjusted neural representation; those representations, taken together, come to be Chicago or a water lily to that person. Linkages among millions or billions of neurons create an inestimable number of representations of Chicago or a water lily, and the more representations there are, the more nuanced, subtle, and layered will be the meaning of those words and the facts, ideas, and feelings they contain. The more numerous, complex, and challenging the information elements received about Chicago are, over time, the more textured will be the meaning made of those representations. It is not just that more input and more representations generate a more detailed understanding of the city; richness in amounts, sources, and types of information, complete with emotional undertones and overtones, result in an increasingly personalized, unique, and meaningful overall portrayal of Chicago in the mind. What happened to someone while in Chicago, which friends or relatives live (or used to live) there, what the weather was like during visits, how Chicago has been portrayed in a novel he or she read, and the images of Chicago seen on television shows and news reports about events there all influence meaning making in very particular and personal ways. So one person's Chicago will never be exactly the same as another's. Chicago, of course, as an objective entity is always Chicago. But our ability to say what the objective characteristics of Chicago are is, for each of us, limited by the net product of our experiences, perceptions, and observations—all of which are represented in linked neuronal circuits in the brain. Note parenthetically that the neurobiological process of cognitive development influences the range of possibilities for the meaning made of data and information received about Chicago, or anything else; a young child may know Chicago as a city a long way away, and an older child might add more factual amplitude to that concrete characterization (e.g., Chicago is a city in Illinois, a long way away, and three million people live there). But consider the multiple layers of meaning in an adolescent's comment that "Chicago is my hometown" and the nuance required to say (and feel), "Chicago—I love that town."

The way the brain works and develops then models the way observable learning works: every learner takes in new information, relates it somehow to other information already gathered, and creates a new formulation of knowledge that is uniquely his or her own. This is entirely consistent with the observations of cognitive psychologists and educators regarding the influence of experience on education.[15] In a form of education more desired than realized today, students who are truly engaged in learning encounter new material—knowledge, perspectives, points of view, creations, performances, events, activities—and make sense of it in relation to their own previous knowledge, perspectives, points of view, creations, performances, events, and activities. In other words, new information is integrated or linked with existing information. Sometimes, processing and reflecting on the new material inspires a significant change in capacities, attitudes, beliefs, or perspectives. "I used to think X, but, having [taken that course], [read that book], [seen that movie], [had that discussion], [done that community service project], now I think Y." Today neuroscientists are studying and locating the structures and mechanisms involved in these processes, including models for predicting attitude change as a result of certain cognitive conflicts (cognitive dissonance). Underlying the layering of information that generates increasingly complex and, sometimes, abstract meanings is the parallel formation of increasingly complex representations of information within the central nervous systems' communication pathways in the cerebral cortex. Brain imaging now provides strong empirical evidence of this, showing how new memories are created and linked with older ones.

As explained in depth in Chapter 3, the developmental changes that occur in children, adolescents, and adults through a plethora of learning experiences do not happen in one mighty leap. The person of the past does not become the person of the future all at once. Instead, the profound changes that arise from the development process occur in sequences and with timing that can be both predictable and unpredictable, often one at a time but sometimes in a flood, and are ordered and organized differently for each person. Yet the conditions for advancement in cognitive development have to be right (many environmental challenges, from poverty to parental attitudes, can undermine those conditions), and the individual has to be an active participant in the process (development does not happen to someone; someone develops). Critical thinking does not emerge as an expert capacity as a result of a single class in high school or college, and the ability to empathically take the perspective of another person does not arise mechanically from a diversity class or single encounter with someone unlike yourself. The developmental changes we hope to see in students' minds, hearts, and attitudes are ultimately built cumulatively, gradually, and collectively from multiple intentional learning experiences, inside and outside schools and classrooms.

State of Mind—or State of Brain—and Learning

Learning, as a process, embraces not just the mind but the brain and the whole person, at any age. Everything that affects the health and well-being of the learner also strengthens or weakens the learning process;

factors that influence well-being affect the state of mind—or, more properly, the state of brain—of learners. Therefore, the state of mind/brain of a learner is a major determinant of the learner's readiness to learn. Correlations exist between the behavior we can observe in students who are learning and what we can see in brain activity during learning. Good teachers at any level of education have long observed that factors other than native intelligence and the qualities of the learning environment affect students' ability to learn. As examples, students who are under stress, worried about a problem at home, ill or injured, or distracted by competing demands for time and focus do not learn as well, or as efficiently, as do students who are not experiencing those constraints—or as efficiently as they themselves would do were they not experiencing such constraints. Therefore, when we attempt to assess the quality of learning, we must always account for and understand the conditions in the learner; students are not friction-free learning systems. Now brain imaging data show with consistency and clarity what is going on at the functional, neurophysiological level when students who have various short- or long-term constraints try to learn.

A growing body of research studies suggests this relationship between the health of an individual (human or other mammal) and the capacity of the brain to function. Depression and stress may reduce that capacity, and treatment of depression, at least in animal models, may restore some or all of it.[16] This observation, if robustly confirmed, would be completely consistent with the observations of clinicians and educators: depression and stress, among other mental health problems, have long been seen as impairments to effective, engaged, and focused learning.

Some of the most significant findings lead to the conclusion that depression—a mental health problem increasingly recognized among college and university students[17]—is associated with significant decreases in the brain's response to stimuli that should prompt learning. In other words, the observed trait of students who are depressed—the flattening of their interest, affect, and attention, which impairs their readiness to learn and the effectiveness of their attempts to learn—is mirrored in neurophysiological studies.

Overall, the effect of depression on cognitive ability and memory performance is substantial; depressed persons seem to require more activation within the same neural networks to maintain a similar level of performance as control subjects during tests of ability to complete working memory tasks—which suggests that depression impairs cognitive capacity because differing brain resources must be recruited and utilized for any given task than those needed for persons without depression.[18] Restoring the full capacity to learn in students with depression requires treatment of their depression by psychotherapy, psychotropic medications, or both; there is no evidence that they can improve their own learning ability by the sheer force of will, just as there is no evidence that threatening a depressed student with negative academic consequences will cause that student to snap out of it and learn better. Depression can thus be understood as both a mental health disorder that causes profound suffering for many students and a learning problem. It is a vivid example of the more general observation that conditions that affect the state of mind—which really means the state of brain—of the learner can have important effects on the quality of learning; the list of those conditions is quite long and includes other mental health disorders, addictions, and prolonged stress, as well as neurological problems such as attention deficit disorder.

Readiness to learn is a complex construct that engages physical, psychological, emotional, social, and, perhaps, spiritual health; other determinants include motivation, the level of expectations set, and the quality of preparation for the learning task. The state of readiness to learn, by influencing the effectiveness and efficiency of learning, affects the quality of learning outcomes, which in turn affect the persistence, achievement, learning, and success of people engaged in any learning experience. Consider, for example, a working adult who is enrolled in community college courses and his or her ability to focus on the material if he or she is distracted by problems at home, concerned about money, or coping with day-to-day stresses inherent in managing a complex life with many competing demands. Imagine how effectively a college student with untreated or inadequately treated depression will learn in his or her courses, given what we know about the effects of depression on cognitive capacity.

The fundamental idea behind the construct of readiness to learn is that intellect—which is not an abstraction—cannot be separated from the brain, the body, or the whole student. Separating mind and body—or life and learning—is infeasible and impossible. All learning—intellectual, developmental, social, and emotional—occurs through the work done in a living, working brain in a living, working human being.

So the recognition and treatment of anxiety and depression, the management of stress, and the improvements in the quality of the learning environment can all be expected to strengthen learning outcomes. Those improvements will not occur through attention to intellectual questions of curriculum and pedagogy alone.

Neuroplasticity: The Key to Learning

Both animal and human brain neurophysiological experiments now also confirm the extraordinary and continuing *plasticity* of brain tissue—that is, the capacity of brain tissue to remain plastic, or malleable, and capable of change.[19] As late as the 1980s, it was commonly believed that brain development stopped when the bones stopped growing and students reached their adult height.[20] It is now exceedingly clear that much brain tissue remains plastic—able to change its structure and/or functioning— far longer than that. The degree of plasticity that is preserved over years varies by brain region. Eventually, cells that control the movement of fingers cannot be successfully redirected toward sensing particular colors, for example; they are no longer plastic enough to make a complete change in the basic nature of their function. But cells in many regions of the brain retain the capacity to change to lesser degrees in both anatomic (structural) and functional ways.

While it has been long known that human beings can learn—acquire and make meaning of knowledge—all the way through their lives, it has only recently been shown that their ability to do so requires that the brain be plastic enough to create new synapses and neural networks. At the level of microscopic anatomy and function, neuroplasticity is the basis of learning. Without it, learning could not occur; if new information could not cause some rewiring or modification of circuits in the brain, no new information would be retained, represented, or processed. The huge variety of inputs that stimulate learning, from reading or listening to a lecture to watching a performance or doing a scientific experiment, all induce various levels of responses in various interconnected parts of the brain. That activity can, if it is sufficiently powerful and sustained, lead to changes in structure and function of the brain.

This distinction between an ordinary, pedestrian kind of learning— characterized by memorization, last-minute cramming for examinations, and content acquisition without reflection or meaning making—and *higher learning*, which demands engagement and inspires positive, beneficial growth and change can be visualized using advanced brain imaging techniques.[21] The former—purely concrete, semantic learning, such as memorization and content acquisition without reflection—does not challenge the brain, especially when it becomes repetitive. Little energy and work are required to accomplish these rote mental tasks. But the latter—higher learning with abstract thinking and making meaning—is far more demanding, both mentally and physiologically. Memorizing lists of facts asks far less of the brain, as it were, than interpreting those facts and exploring their implications.

The laboratory research results and brain imaging data provide equally convincing evidence of these ideas. Experiments that show differences in the patterns of brain activity as students (or other people) develop expertise in certain fields provide a corollary to how we understand higher education. Unskilled, unpracticed individuals attempting to draw an object or person have very different patterns of brain activation than do experienced artists. In the brains of experienced artists, little work is done in the process of handling a pencil or pen to make the drawing; most of their mental investment occurs far away, in the frontal lobes, where we imagine, dream, wonder, and think about the meaning of things we have seen or experienced.[22] The unskilled artist's brain images exhibit little frontal lobe activity and we see a great deal of oxygen and sugar consumption instead in the motor cortex, where the brain controls the motor processes of writing and drawing. Over time—but only with sufficient time on task (practice!)—the unskilled artists may improve their drawing skills and begin to infuse more meaning into the planning and execution of their drawings; if so, we will see less activation in the motor areas and more in the frontal lobes, as is true of the developed efficiency in the brains of experts. Over time, the brain not only learns certain content or knowledge, but also learns how to use its own resources as efficiently as possible—repeated processes gain what is called "automaticity."[23] These results had been anticipated in theory long before they were proven in practice; Sigmund Freud articulated the concept that the process of learning changes the grid of electrical activity in the human brain without being able to use today's technologies to visualize what this actually meant in terms of brain structure and function.[24]

Conclusion

The educational implications of these neurobiological observations about brain functioning during learning are sharp and clear: they confirm that the deep, engaged form of learning that we call *higher learning* is associated not only with changes in brain structure and function, but also with the development of greater knowledge and skill in specific areas of expertise. The salient, positive changes that we hope to see from students' engagement with higher education then require sufficient time on task and immersion in learning tasks to prompt successive reorderings of the brain's neural networks. The achievement of sufficient time on task and immersion in learning tasks in turn requires motivation, commitment, and the willingness to give priority to academic work—in other words, higher expectations of students' performance and of teachers' creativity and investment in teaching.[25] Drifting through college may get one a degree, unfortunately, but it does not secure any degree of *higher learning*, and it is unlikely to produce expertise in any area.

Students who wish to attain high levels of expertise in any area are obligated to study, review, practice, and study, review, and practice again, and again. Trivial levels of engagement with new material—achieved in the midnight revelry of memorizing a list of essential facts with which to pass an exam the next morning—are unlikely to result in the transfer of information to long- term memory and to achieve sustained changes in the brain, do not stick, and cannot be expected to generate expertise. Most of those facts are quickly forgotten. Deep engagement with content, the creation of new knowledge through research, assiduous and diligent practice, and cultural immersion (for example, in international study) are examples of methods of engaged learning that can be reasonably expected to achieve substantial changes in the brain.

5

Assessment of Higher Learning

The "A" Words: Assessment and Accountability

Our collective anxiety over the value received in return for so much public and private investment has reached new heights, given the lack of systematic evidence of higher learning among undergraduates in American colleges and universities. With this anxiety comes a demand for greater accountability: accrediting bodies and state legislatures have put pressure on institutions of higher education of all types to produce more and better data that document the quality and quantity of student learning. Such demands have rendered assessment and accountability the most pejorative and despised of "A" words in the lexicon of higher education.

Many faculty members have resisted calls for accountability based on student learning, pointing to the damage that the imposition of accountability requirements has inflicted on primary and secondary schools. They note that as educators in K–12 schools have been asked with increasing frequency and intensity to demonstrate greater accountability, there has been a concurrent rise in institutional cheating, a narrowing of intended learning outcomes, an increase in charges of teaching to the test, and a lowering of state standards to improve pass rates. They fear that coming generations of high school graduates will come to college even less prepared than their predecessors for conceptual, critical, and abstract thinking.

These faculty members have a point; attempts to respond to the need for evidence of learning have too often gone astray, and sometimes magnificently so. Since 2002, for example, we have endured the imposition of No Child Left Behind (NCLB) in primary and secondary education, a federally mandated program that relies heavily on standardized testing of reading and mathematics for the purpose of accountability yet has been unable to provide data that clearly and consistently document any significant learning gains. NCLB has generated bureaucracies, rewarded the developers and purveyors of standardized tests, taken the focus off long-term learning goals, and reduced the flexibility with which primary and secondary school teachers can cover their material in ways customized to the needs of individual children and classes. NCLB has not, however, produced more qualified high school graduates who are more likely to succeed in college.

Indeed, the legitimate demand for accountability for learning at the K–12 level illustrated by NCLB has had certain perverse, unintended effects for several reasons, including the application of ill-conceived criteria and standards, the use of inappropriate incentives and punishments for teachers and individual schools, and the misapplication of standardized tests. Standardized tests are important for comparability and consistency, but the good ones—that is, the tests that reliably measure student's progress toward desired learning goals, such as the Collegiate Learning Assessment (CLA), Programme for International Student Assessment (PISA), and National Assessment of Educational Progress (NAEP)—require rigor in development and are, accordingly, more expensive. Most of the more affordable, state-approved standardized tests used in K-12 education emphasize recall of facts, not assessment of the achievement of broad learning goals. Cost-consciousness in many public school districts governs the selection of tests, and the use of tests that primarily measure factual knowledge, plus the pressure on teachers, principals, and superintendents to achieve good results, has led teachers and students alike to focus on "what students have to know to pass the test" rather than promoting critical thinking, problem solving, and other long-term, cumulative learning goals. Politicians, the media, and educators themselves have worsened the situation by, often unwittingly, using assessments in unfortunate and counterproductive ways—such as anointing winners and castigating losers.

Demands for greater institutional accountability in higher education also have led to calls for improved graduation rates and higher levels of productivity—and not just among administrators. Questions about how faculty members spend their time and what level of teaching loads should be expected of them are now discussed in legislative committees and the press; in at least one state, a governor has insisted that professors in state institutions teach one more class each per academic year. In the tense atmosphere created by these discussions, it is no wonder that faculty members and academic administrators express cynicism about the value of accountability-driven measures of learning and fear the arrival of similar methods in higher education.

Still, the bad experience to date with accountability demands placed on K–12 does not negate the imperative to assess learning. Assessment can and should be a powerful form of teaching and learning. Done in an appropriate and timely way, assessment is a necessary condition for improving learning at all levels of education and can be constructively construed and implemented in ways that can strengthen teaching, improve learning, and, yes, respond more effectively to calls for accountability. Research convincingly demonstrates that learning is powerfully aided by feedback, to both students and teachers, during (formative) and at the completion of (summative) instruction. These benefits do not accrue from just any kind of feedback delivered at just any time or in just any manner; feedback that has impact must stem from assessment that is appropriate to the task, timely, and transparent. Assessment of this caliber improves learning and augments student success. Furthermore, accountability for learning becomes a shared responsibility among students, professors, and the institution.[1]

For colleges and universities, learning assessment is an essential way of making the quality and quantity of learning visible. Assessment gives an institution data, and those data not only help identify and remove barriers to higher learning among students, but also enable the improvement of educational programs at all levels, from whole curricula to individual learning experiences inside or outside the classroom. The most effective data come from assessments based on clear statements of learning goals, objectives, standards, and criteria of excellence against which learning will be measured. Maximum transparency of these goals and criteria allows faculty members to share the task of teaching for learning across courses and programs and, at the same time, intentionally signals to students what is expected of them and how their performance—evidence of their learning—will be judged. Taking the guesswork out by providing clear objectives and standards is the foundation for providing necessary and timely feedback in a formative, diagnostic manner to both students and teachers during the process of learning. Feedback arms students with a more adequate and accurate sense of how well they are meeting learning objectives in ways that sustain and enrich learning itself. Feedback also allows room for remediation and reteaching. In the aggregate, the content of feedback delivered to students helps professors and other educators understand the effectiveness of their pedagogy. Moreover, feedback signals and reinforces faculty members' expected standards of achievement, allowing them to work with students toward a shared goal. In short, assessment can and should serve a fundamental function—as support *for* learning. Such learning, and the assessment of that learning, serves the need for accountability that matters most.

Arguments against Assessment

The professoriate has often resisted calls for learning-based accountability. Educated in graduate school to be scholars in their disciplines, but receiving little or no training in teaching or learning, faculty members have been, for the most part, indoctrinated into an institutional culture deeply rooted in a "publish or perish" reward system. Few were hired with any expectation that the quality and quantity of learning in their courses would be measured, or that learning would be a criterion for promotion and tenure. To the extent that they are prepared to address teaching and learning at all, most faculty members think in terms of the quality of teaching (how well they perform as instructors), not that of learning (how well students acquire, make meaning of, and can integrate and apply knowledge) as a result of their teaching.

Although arguments against accountability can sometimes be explained by the fear of challenge and change, faculty members also offer reasons for their opposition that deserve review and consideration: that the most important learning during the college years cannot be measured, that too few good learning measures exist, that reliable and valid assessment is too time-consuming and detracts from instruction (and therefore from the teaching of needed content), and that it is impossible to differentiate the contributions of teachers from the vagaries of student motivation and from the effects of their diverse backgrounds. In other words, measuring what matters has been inverted; professors now charge that what we can measure must not matter and that what matters can never be measured. There are just concerns among these reasons, and there are solid, legitimate responses to them as well. While concern about our ability to assess learning effectively can and should generate sound discourse about the best ways in which to do so in a variety of disciplines and settings, the *status quo* takes us dangerously close to the famous *reductio ad absurdum:* "No matter, never mind."

Faculty members do, however, already practice assessment in limited but ubiquitous ways. They assess students' acquisition of disciplinary content in their own courses—papers, quizzes, midterms, and finals are the standard methods, and the use of portfolios, comprehensive examinations, and capstone courses is increasing across campuses nationwide. Seldom, if ever, are those methods of assessment used to evaluate anything other than students' performance against professors' standards; it is rare, even in today's climate of rampant grade inflation, that a professor is seriously criticized or a course changed because too many students got low grades in that course. When that happens, students simply choose not to take that course, or any other course from that professor, but the course itself does not change. Bad grades are assumed to be evidence of poor student performance; the possibility that they represent a poorly designed or delivered learning experience is nearly inconceivable.

Evaluation at the end of courses is understood and accepted by students and faculty as normative and necessary to provide grades and award credit in a system in which credit hours and seat time serve as the surrogates for actual evidence of learning. The faculty is legitimately concerned that assessing learning at the end of college, in standardized ways that are determined by others outside the academy, will foster unwarranted homogeneity and reinforce the development and imposition of a compliance-based ethic that reduces learning to something that can be easily measured with the type of standardized, short-answer tests born under NCLB.[2] Indeed, given the inadequate state of assessment tools at both institutional and cross-institutional levels, the lack of faculty training in either teaching or assessment, and a system generally skewed against both, the quest for accountability for the quality and quantity of learning—especially for externally imposed accountability and even more for comparative accountability—is an uphill battle.

Measuring What We Value

Robust assessment of students' ability to integrate knowledge and of the achievement of transformational learning that we associate with higher education is not part of mainstream instruction within or across courses and years in college.[3] As a result, institutions can provide almost no useful evidence of learning that demonstrates the effective and successful application of their own teaching mission. In addition, institutions have little ability to respond to calls for accountability for the quality and quantity of student learning.

One common response is that the job market is the real test. "Our students are being hired and doing well," administrators and faculty members may say. That explanation has had diminished resonance lately as a college degree no longer guarantees employment and as employers have become increasingly critical of the competence, flexibility, and resilience of college graduates. Given the stated purpose of colleges and universities as learning institutions, how can accounting for student learning be given such short shrift?

Testing takes place, but usually at a point at which it is too late for feedback to be useful (classically, at the end of a course) and rarely at a level of sophistication that does justice to higher learning. How can a student who received an F for her performance in a course based primarily on the work she did on a term paper and/or her performance on the final examination go back and improve her work? Motivated mostly by the desire to complete their courses and get a degree, rather than by any true engagement with learning, many students only check their grades—but rarely review comments on papers or final exams (if there are any) that might have guided improvements in their performance. This is especially true (and, to a degree, understandable) if there is no opportunity to improve because there is no next paper or examination.

Note further that testing, as an assessment strategy, usually does not measure the extent to which students have made meaning of new material or experiences, leveraged the new knowledge they have acquired, integrated that new knowledge with what they have learned before, or grown in their ability to understand or take the perspective of others— testing usually doesn't measure the significant outcomes of higher learning. Poorly designed tests fail even to adequately assess comprehension;

such tests only determine whether the student has committed information to memory for long enough to relay that information back on a single occasion. This is incongruous with how we robustly assess students' learning of new knowledge and skills in preparing them for endeavors we truly value, such as cardiopulmonary resuscitation (CPR), flying an airplane, scuba diving, or performing robotic microsurgery. Just remembering the steps in CPR—"airway, breathing, circulation"—won't cut it; we need to see that students have been able to put new knowledge and techniques into their own hands. Hence we develop finely tailored, challenging, and competency-based assessments of students' learning of these highly valued sets of knowledge and skills.

Consider the assessments of learning among surgeons, pilots, and military officers who are still in training. Neither learning nor its assessment is left to chance. We insist upon high, clear, and well-documented standards for judging expertise in these cases; there are no secrets about what is expected or how success at meeting those expectations will be measured. Measurement, in fact, becomes an inextricable part of instruction and promotion through not only objective tests, but also simulations, comprehensive written and oral examinations, and proof of performance. These assessments are completely competency based; students do not move to the next level of training without clearly demonstrating at least satisfactory performance on the previous level. None of us would consider flying with a pilot who has not been fully trained and tested on takeoffs and landings—nor would we tolerate having an operation performed by a surgeon who had not been adequately certified by the training program and an examining board, or having a root canal performed by an uncertified endodontist. No branch of the armed forces entrusts the deployment and leadership of troops to untested or poorly performing officers; in fact, testing is how leaders in any of the armed services know which officers perform well and therefore which ones to trust. In other words, when it really matters, we find ways to do timely, meaningful assessment of learning.

But if the time, energy, and money invested in the enterprise are any indication, we do genuinely value higher education in this country. We presume that colleges and universities are effective because (1) they claim to design and implement learning experiences that support students' acquisition, application, and adaptation of new knowledge and abilities in preparation for life, citizenship, and work, and (2) they employ faculty members who, by virtue of their own terminal degrees, are presumed to have the capacity to teach effectively. Yet, little evidence exists to substantiate these claims and their effectiveness. Since 2000, the National Center for Public Policy and Higher Education has provided grades of F (failing) and I (incomplete) to states to denote the lack of proof of effectiveness—or of the existence of data that might provide proof one way or the other—of learning in higher education.[4] The Lumina Foundation sums up the assessment of learning that is now happening on most campuses as follows: "There is too little credible data to justify the quality distinctions that are often made in higher education. We simply aren't doing enough to measure the specific learning that takes place in individual courses and degree programs. In most cases, we can't really tell what value an institution truly adds to its students' lives."[5]

This scarcity of data is more than troubling, and it has serious public policy ramifications as well. The increasing concern that college graduates do not write or speak well, cannot think critically, and too often graduate with a lack of self-discipline or the humility of knowing that there is much one does not know has led to an appropriate increase in anxiety over and demand for accountability and evidence of value. As the academy struggles with issues of cost and accessibility, its historical credibility as an assumed public good is eroding.

How, then, might the conflicting demands for the assessment of learning as a means of improving instruction and as an expression of institutional accountability be reconciled? And how might we do so without having the discussion become overly politicized, on and off campus, as it has happened in the K–12 sector? We must begin by creating a normative campus culture that views assessment as a form of teaching and learning in and of itself and accepts a shared responsibility for accountability based on institutionwide measures of learning.

Developing a Culture of Assessment: A Model

The shift to a culture of assessment may be initially threatening to institutions (and faculty), but it is also potentially transforming. Such a shift has been successfully implemented in certain areas of health care, one of which was elegantly described in *The New Yorker* in 2004 by Dr. Atul

Gawande, professor of surgery at the Harvard Medical School. Dr. Gawande describes different ways of treating patients with cystic fibrosis and relates those to the patients' rates of survival across the very best hospitals and clinics in this country.[6] He notes that the results were distributed on a bell curve; patients at an average treatment center lived to be just over 30 years old, but similar patients at the center with the best results typically lived to be 46. Clearly this is a difference that matters! But what causes that difference, and how did Gawande bring it to light?

The perceived reputation and rankings of hospitals and clinics often compiled by popular magazines do not predict successful outcomes for treating cystic fibrosis. Effective treatment, Gawande found, results from the cumulative and collective efforts of the patient, the patient's family, physicians, hospital staff, and others. Success requires quality care from doctors, but also compliance by patients with daily physical therapy and breathing exercises, the continuous monitoring of lung capacity, and the prescription (and utilization) of appropriate medications. In sum, the most effective hospitals have figured out ways of teaching patients, their families, and staff members how best to partner in treating this condition. Their solution demands ongoing assessment and requires continuous feedback to staff members, as well as patients and their families; it is an ongoing conversation among everyone involved in patient care.

The fundamental component of the most effective treatment for cystic fibrosis is a caring and demanding hospital culture that requires rigorous and transparent measurement of outcomes and the sharing of findings in a timely manner. Formative assessment data inform and improve compliance by patients and families and aid physicians in their constant efforts to improve treatment. Summative data provide grounds for improvement via institutional benchmarking—how well are we doing as an institution compared to others like us? The point of such benchmarking is not to provide fodder for boasting; it is to ensure that the patients in medical center A have as good an outcome as do those treated in medical center B.

Making treatment outcome data public leaves clinics with no alternative but to do everything possible to help patients survive, even while being candid creates the risk of being challenged. But with such risk comes great benefit—the ability to recalibrate criteria for excellence and establish a culture of continuous improvement. As one doctor put it,

"There is no place to hide; this is like going naked."[7] A culture of assessment, then, based on a commitment to transparency and continuous feedback to the patient, manifests itself in significant and powerful real-life outcomes.

We in the academy are populated with "doctors" as well, and the quality of "treatment" of the hearts and minds of students is very much in our hands. An institutional culture of assessment in the academy can assure excellence and effectiveness, just as it does in medicine. With such impetus, we suggest six central attributes of a culture of assessment that higher education should strive to institute to attain such excellence and effectiveness: transparency, the use of standards-based criteria, cumulative and collective learning, formative as well as summative assessment, authentic assessment methods and reporting, and benchmarking. No one of these will be sufficient in and of itself, but taken together and applied in the aggregate, they can improve the quality and quantity of learning in higher education.

Transparency: Opening Up the Black Box

What would "going naked" mean in higher education? Fundamentally, it would mean that faculty members—in partnership with others who educate students, including student affairs professionals—define and measure the quality of learning in all forms and venues far more consistently, openly, and thoroughly than is now the norm on most campuses. That, in turn, would require that every institution and each of its colleges and schools, and all of their divisions and departments, establish common expectations for what students should know and what skills they should have when they complete a given program of study[8] and the levels of mastery they should attain at various intervals within a program. This is no simple charge, since a program of study may comprise a single classroom or experiential learning activity, a course, the cluster of courses that constitute a core curriculum, and the courses and experiences that make up a major. The program of study is any intentional learning experience, or set of experiences, that has specific intended learning outcomes that can be assessed.

Faculty members implicitly know what they are trying to measure and generally believe they know how they will judge quality, but their expectations and standards are usually not explicitly translated to students in advance, and they change from course to course and professor to professor. Students often complain that they do not clearly understand what they are expected to learn; it is, then, unsurprising that asking, "Will it be on the test?" becomes their method of ascertaining expectations. Resentment and cries of capricious grading result and affirm the truth of Robert Pirsig's observation: "If you can't say what quality is . . . then for all practical purposes it doesn't exist at all."[9] Students taught by a professor who does not specify what they are expected to learn are left to read the professor's mind as they prepare for class, write papers, and take exams. In this situation, one might argue that students are being graded not on the basis of their learning, but instead on their ability to psych out their professor. The ability to do so may have little to do with intended learning outcomes.

Effectively supporting good student learning requires that professors define and communicate the intended objectives for each course, including the nature of the learning assessments to be utilized and the standards and criteria that will be used for judging learning, all in advance. There should be no surprises. Making students guess what matters most, how competency will be assessed, or what the criteria for various levels of accomplishment are serves no educational purpose. Moreover, a culture of assessment requires that faculty members share their expectations— and the results of their learning assessments—with both their students and their colleagues, since higher learning is based on collectively determined goals and outcomes. In addition, such sharing and transparency support the cumulative achievement of those goals and outcomes that results only from the aggregate of the teaching and learning that occur in many contexts across the institution.

Standards-Based Assessment

Standards-based assessment—in which students' performance is assessed against a known, transparent standard, rather than in comparison to the performance of other students—will best support higher learning. But both students and faculty are far more used to—and often more comfortable with—norm-referenced assessments, which are based on comparisons with the performance of other students. In particular, course grades are often curved. A student giving exactly the same performance in two different situations may receive different grades if the performance of other students in those two situations varies substantially. In other words, a student's work will look better or worse depending on the context created by the work of other students. Furthermore, the whole curve may move up or down on a grading scale depending on professors' dispositions; in an environment of grade inflation, the whole curve moves upward and the distribution of grades is skewed toward higher marks. While there are limited, though cogent, arguments in favor of curved grading, norm-referenced assessment has limited usefulness for individual students because high grades do not necessarily denote competence.

The limitations of norm-referenced assessment become painfully clear when we consider how we measure competency in high-risk areas. Suppose the assessment of prospective airline pilots utilized norm-referenced testing, and pilot candidates had to demonstrate satisfactory performance on four fundamental skills: takeoffs; right-hand turns; left-hand turns; and landings. Now suppose one candidate received 100 percent on takeoffs, 100 percent on left-hand turns, 100 percent on right-hand turns, and 75 percent on landings, giving her a 94 percent average (which is generally an A grade), and placing her in the highest percentile of all those taking the same test. A fellow student who got 100 percent on takeoffs, 75 percent on left-hand turns, 75 percent on right-hand turns, and 100 percent on landings would have gotten 87.5 percent—usually a B. But the second student would have landed the plane every time.

Would you fly with the first pilot? No way! You would say she wasn't competent because she had not met a standard that we all hold as the minimum—100 percent on landings. Suppose, however, that we first established absolute standards or criteria for competence, such as a 100 percent criterion for successful takeoffs and landings, that are not referenced to the performance of other trainees. The critical issue would then be how well the trainee did against clearly defined standards set in advance, not how well one candidate did against others. As an airline passenger, you don't care how other students did on landings; you only care—and rightly so—that your pilot scored 100 percent on landings.

This is criterion-referenced or standards-based assessment, and it focuses on measuring knowledge and skills against such standards—whether airplane takeoffs and landings, knowledge and understanding of biology, critical thinking and writing skills, or the ability to use calculus in solving engineering problems. Standards-based assessment is not sensitive to variations in competency levels among groups of students; a given student will get the same grade whether tested as part of a high-performing group or a low-performing one. All students can get As or Fs; judgment of competence is made against clear and explicit criteria, not simply against the chance distribution of other talent in the classroom.

For standards-based assessment to work, educators must guide students' learning toward acquiring the knowledge and skills required to satisfy the criteria that define competency. For such direction of learning to occur, teachers must carefully define the learning objectives for courses (or other learning experiences), tell students what those objectives are, and offer a curriculum and use teaching methods that will facilitate students' learning. Taken together, those steps comprise a tightly coupled system of instruction. Coupling desired learning outcomes, pedagogy, curriculum, assessment methods and standards, and sharing these with students prior to instruction, signals what is expected of everyone involved in the learning process—no more guessing or mind reading!

How would such a tightly coupled system actually work? Faculty members, having defined what they wanted students to learn, would draw up criteria with which they would assess students' learning and share those criteria with students and colleagues. Suppose, for example, faculty members in different academic departments wanted to be sure that students, regardless of their major, learned to think critically and write effectively. Those faculty members would work together to define the characteristics of critical thinking and effective writing that they wanted to see demonstrated in their students; those characteristics would become the criteria on which the faculty would assess the quality of student learning in those areas. Where diversity would occur is in the instruction toward and assessment of such common objectives. Students would learn the specific knowledge, concepts, principles, and problems unique to each discipline/course/program in which those objectives are addressed. Standards for accuracy and adequacy within each field necessarily must be determined by experts in those fields. But in each field, and with each focused on its own base of knowledge, faculty would teach and assess students' achievement of the common learning goals of critical thinking and effective writing.

following list is a series of questions that might be asked by faculty members across disciplines as they define what they, in common, expect of students studying within any and all disciplines.[10] Questions such as these informed the developers of the nationally used Collegiate Learning Assessment (CLA) but can also serve as a model for constructing a general set of standards that faculty members in individual institutions can tailor to assess students' knowledge, concepts, and principles in their own disciplinary areas. Notice, as you review the questions, that they try to answer the question, "How would you know it when you see it?" That is, they provide a practical, grounded method for determining whether students have achieved the desired learning goals with enough consistency to permit the equitable assessment of outcomes among many different students. Note as well that these criteria may be applied across the many courses, programs, and disciplines found in higher education.[11]

Critical Thinking

Evaluation of evidence: How well does the student assess the quality and relevance of evidence?

- Does the student determine what information is or is not pertinent to the task at hand?
- Does the student distinguish between rational claims and emotional ones, fact from opinion?
- Can the student recognize the ways in which the evidence might be limited or compromised?
- Does the student spot deception and holes in the arguments of others?
- Has the student considered all sources of evidence?

Analysis and synthesis of evidence: How well does the student analyze and synthesize data and information?

- Does the student present his or her own analysis of the data or information, or does he or she simply present it as is?
- Does the student commit or fail to recognize logical flaws in an argument. (e.g., does the student understand the distinction between correlation and causation)?
- Does the student break down the evidence into its component parts?

- Does the student draw connections between discrete sources of data and information?
- How does the student deal with conflicting, inadequate, or ambiguous information?

Drawing conclusions: How well does the student form a conclusion from his or her analysis?

- Is the student's argument logically sound?
- Is it rooted in data and information rather than speculation and opinion?
- Does the student choose the strongest set of data to support his or her argument?
- Does the student prioritize in his or her argumentation?
- Does the student overstate, or understate, his or her conclusions?
- Can the student identify holes in the evidence and subsequently suggest additional information that might resolve the issue?

Acknowledging alternative explanations/viewpoints: How well does the student consider other options and acknowledge that her or his answer is not the only perspective?

- Does the student recognize that the problem is complex with no clear answer?
- Does the student bring up other options and weigh them in her or his decision?
- Does the student consider all stakeholders or affected parties in suggesting a course of action?
- Does the student qualify his or her response and acknowledge the need for additional information in making an absolute determination?

Writing

Presentation: How clear and concise is the argument?

- Does the student clearly articulate the argument?
- Does the student clearly articulate the context for that argument?
- Is the evidence used to defend the argument correct and precise?

- Is the evidence presented in a comprehensible and coherent fashion?

Development: How effective is the structure?

- Is the organization of the argument logical? Is it cohesive?
- Are there any gaps in the development of the argument?
- Are there any significantly extraneous elements in the argument's development?
- In what order is the evidence presented, and how does that structure contribute to the persuasiveness and coherence of the argument?

Persuasiveness: How well does the student defend the argument?

- What evidence is presented in support of the argument, and how effectively does the student present it?
- Does the student draw thoroughly and extensively from the available range of evidence?
- How well does the student analyze that evidence?
- Does the student consider counterarguments and address weaknesses in his or her own argument?

Mechanics: What is the quality of the student's writing?

- Is vocabulary and punctuation used correctly and effectively?
- Is the student's understanding of grammar strong?
- Is the sentence structure basic or more complex and creative?
- Does the student use proper transitions?
- Are the paragraphs structured logically and effectively?

Interest: How well does the student maintain the reader's interest?

- Does the student use creative and engaging examples or descriptions?
- Does the structure syntax and organization add to the interest of his or her writing?
- Does the student use colorful but relevant metaphors, similes, and so on?
- Does the writing engage the reader?
- Does the writing leave the reader thinking?

Such criteria act as standards that signal to students what is considered important. Students attempting to write well would know, for example, that vocabulary, sentence structure, and grammar are all elements of good writing, and, over time, would learn to assess their own work in progress against those criteria. As students submit their written work for assessment in a succession of courses taught by a variety of faculty members, they develop increasingly accurate definitions of proper transitions or logical paragraph structure in their own minds. Tools such as these can eventually help students judge for themselves how well they are learning, without having to rely solely on feedback from the teacher. Of equal importance, the development of such shared criteria allows faculty members, individually and collectively, to more carefully and reliably offer both formative and summative feedback to students across courses and disciplines.

Note, in the sample lists that each major characteristic desired in a student's writing or critical thinking is associated with a group of "know it when you see it" examples. How would you know whether a student's writing was persuasive, for example? One looks for the evidence that the student presents, the sources of evidence that were used, how well that evidence is analyzed, and whether counter arguments are considered. The combination of desired characteristics and those "know it when you see it" points allows faculty to create rubrics—structured criteria that serve as tools to assist teachers in assessing students' learning in a consistent manner. Examples of such rubrics developed by faculty may be found in the Association of American Colleges and Universities (AAC&U) VALUE (Valid Assessment of Learning in Undergraduate Education) project.[12] Creating, distributing, and explaining rubrics to students facilitates the development of their capacity for self-assessment and reduces or eliminates any mystery associated with the feedback they receive from faculty.

The use of formative, standards-based assessment would bring significant change in higher education. At the individual classroom level, it would enable faculty members to better communicate their teaching intentions and standards of excellence to both students and their faculty colleagues. It would also make public the nature of individual faculty expectations and help mitigate grade inflation. At the institutional level, measuring cumulative learning in both general education and in the majors would allow institutions to compare themselves with similarly situated peers and thus better benchmark their own expectations, standards, and results. In state systems of colleges and universities, standards-based assessment would change the funding formulae from the current full-time equivalent (FTE) student scheme to one that would require evidence of student learning through consistent assessments against clear standards of excellence defined and provided by the campus. How many students an institution had enrolled would not matter; how much those students learned would matter a great deal. For both private and public colleges and universities, standards-based assessment would mean substituting learning rather than retention as the ultimate criterion of institutional and student success. And given that a majority of students now attend more than one college or university on their way to an undergraduate degree, measures of their learning rather than credit hours or the titles of courses would become the currency of quality. In making such changes, learning, clearly and consistently defined and measured by each institution, would become the hallmark for both internal and external accountability.

Cumulative and Collective Learning

As in the example of optimum care for people with cystic fibrosis discussed earlier, the successful treatment of most other serious medical problems is the cumulative result of the collective efforts of patients, doctors, nurses, hospital staff, and families. Similarly, hallmarks of higher learning such as critical thinking, coherent and persuasive writing and speaking, appreciating differing perspectives, and developing ethical principles are the cumulative results of the efforts of professors and students across many learning experiences and several years. No one course in writing, critical thinking, or moral reasoning, for example, can accomplish such ends because developing competence may require hundreds of opportunities for instruction, practice, and feedback, formally and informally, in and out of the classroom. Students do not learn to think critically by writing one paper, rehearsing one argument in a class, or defending one point of view in a residence hall conversation. Higher learning requires many varied opportunities for practice and feedback— unfortunately, a far cry from what passes for college level work now.

Cumulative and collective higher learning requires, by nature, that faculty members identify shared learning outcomes and criteria for excellence, in advance and across the disciplines. Implicit in doing so is an understanding that each is responsible for teaching to and assessing such outcomes. Faculty members—not external agencies—can do this best, because faculty-developed measures of learning have high context validity.[13] This means that the measures of learning are developed from the specific goals, methods, and activities through which a particular faculty member provides learning experiences for his or her own students. Thus professors in physics, psychology, sociology, and literature, for example, would all teach critical thinking and excellent writing within their own disciplines because they collectively expect students in that college or university to graduate having mastered such outcomes across many instances required for the development of such cumulatively learned and collectively espoused competence. The developers of the CLA suggest that faculty members adapt the criteria used in the CLA for their own courses and curricula. Content knowledge and skill mastery are developed over time, across courses, by students and professors building and integrating learning that gradually and incrementally becomes more complex, sophisticated, and satisfying.

Similar to what Etienne Wenger refers to as "communities of practice," this approach creates close professional partnerships with others who share similar expectations and criteria for excellence.[14] Although we often think of apprenticeship as a relationship between a student and a master, Wenger notes that further elaboration of that concept as it is applied to higher education reveals a more complex set of social relationships through which significant learning takes place. Masters, journeymen, and advanced apprentices are all integral parts of the equation as "groups of people who share a concern or a passion for something they do and learn how to do better as they interact regularly."[15] Over time and with sustained interaction, they develop a sense of shared practice. In short, collective and cumulative learning requires purposeful connection to many others as members joined as a learning community in a common endeavor. A learning community focused on effective writing or critical thinking might engage faculty from several disciplines, graduate assistants who work with those faculty members in their courses, and undergraduates who are dedicated to improving their own writing and, perhaps, to mentoring their peers.

The problem is that faculty members are trained in particular cultures of scholarly disciplines, each with its own language, facts, principles, concepts, frames of reference, and ways of knowing that students are expected to master on their own. Individual autonomy is the cultural norm in higher education, even within disciplines and departments. There is, in general, no expectation or need to share common content or skill objectives or to be held collectively responsible for learning that spans more than one course. Despite frequent claims that general education courses are linked and integrated, students generally move through a disparate collection of classes chosen somehow from lists of courses that satisfy certain requirements, in which the content of each course is unrelated to that offered in any other classes.

Developing and implementing an actual core curriculum is an alternative that requires something very different. A core curriculum builds upon agreement among faculty from different disciplines about where and how certain shared learning goals should be addressed and assessed. Reaching such agreement is not easy. So a smorgasbord of distribution requirements (specifying that students must take some number of courses in each of several areas of study, such as humanities, natural sciences, and social sciences) has replaced core programs for general education, and students, usually without the benefit of consistent and substantial advising, must discern the relationships among these classes and make their learning coherent and cumulative on their own. But without mentoring and guidance, most do not make these connections and are not asked to connect and integrate their learning across many different settings. As explained in the first two chapters of this book, the higher learning we value occurs too often by chance, if and when it occurs at all. Students are often left to flounder from course to course, wondering what these required classes could possibly have to do with each other, or with their life and career goals.

Yet there does not have to be a conflict between faculty autonomy and the need for collective responsibility for cumulative learning. One can respect and honor the freedom to teach specific disciplinary content and utilize tailored strategies to impart that content, while at the same time respecting and honoring the expectations that students will learn to think critically and write well within and across those various disciplines. Sharing a commitment to collective, cumulative outcomes does not mean that professors become automatons, nor does it undermine the extraordinary heterogeneity of teaching styles that allow professors to appeal to and inspire students in their own distinctive ways.

Formative Assessment

When higher learning is understood as a developmental, transformative process centered in the construction of meaning, the concept of formative assessment takes on new and critical importance. It is not simply students' errors that matter, but also how students respond to those errors and to feedback they receive about their errors. This is not unfamiliar: in our professional lives, how we respond to negative reviews of our performance, failed projects or experiments, rejected manuscripts, and unaccepted or unfunded grant proposals has real consequence. We must respond constructively to error and critique (even—and perhaps especially—when we think we were right, and the critique is wrong) to improve our work and move on. We accept, then, a broad principle of quality improvement in our own work; we do the best we can, submit the work we did for review, and accept—hopefully with grace—comments and recommendations for improving it. Inherent in this way of thinking are the belief that each of us benefits from the ideas of others and an affirmation of the idea of progressive refinement of ideas and intellectual products through cycles of review and reworking. We understand that the processes of creating good academic work are iterative, by nature.

But this is not necessarily the case on campus. Most testing in colleges and universities has taught students to provide *right* answers, and learning has become about getting the most *right* answers on a test. Summative assessment alone—that final evaluation and/or grade received at the end of a course—arrives too late to offer helpful feedback. Yet most college-level assessment is summative. Until recently, there was little effort by most professors to use formative assessment in ways that support the cycles of review and reworking that are essential to progressive improvements in fundamental cognitive skills such as critical thinking or good writing. Formative or just-in-time assessment is key—timely, appropriate, and transparent assessment during instruction that provides feedback to both teacher and student and improves both student learning and teaching.[16] Think of it this way: formative assessment is the process of gathering information about the quality and quantity of learning while it is occurring. Formative assessment is really a form of pedagogy; it can range from formal feedback on first, second, or third drafts of a paper to short diagnostic quizzes or even verbal reactions from peers and/or the instructor during classroom discussions. Regardless of the method and format, formative assessment provides feedback to students that includes examples of what is expected, standards against which they'll be judged, opportunities to learn and develop, and opportunities to improve self-assessment skills.

Formative assessment can only reap such benefits if individual faculty members find that it can be done practically, has the support of their colleagues, and contributes to their development as professionals. Incorporating substantial formative learning assessment thus requires broader reform, including rebalancing faculty incentives and rewards to recognize demonstrated student learning as a criterion for promotion and tenure equal to maintaining a research program and getting publications in peer-reviewed journals. Otherwise, tenure-track faculty members may well think that the extra effort required—and extra effort is in fact required—to do frequent formative assessment in classes is not worth it.

Authentic Assessment

One approach to measuring learning explicitly links what students are learning in college to the practical knowledge and life skills they will be required to demonstrate after graduation. Such authentic assessment directly examines students' competence in performing worthy tasks and asks them to apply what they have learned in real world situations.[17] At the crux of authentic assessment are measurements of what are fundamentally transferable cognitive skills—for example, thinking and writing skills learned in college that are important for competency in the world of work, service, and citizenship.

Authentic assessments might ask students to determine the reliability of information obtained from various sources; prove the primacy of competing claims on intellectual, civic, or social matters; offer evidence in support of a point of view; develop new knowledge through research; communicate or present information to audiences; or collaborate with others in solving problems. As is true of other approaches to assessment, clear criteria that are well documented and explained to students in advance are essential.

Benchmarking

How do we know whether we as individuals, programs, academic departments, student affairs divisions, or whole institutions of higher education are doing our best work? Given that we want to achieve excellence in our own work, how will we know it when we see it? How will we know that we are doing as well as, or not as well as, other institutions? If we were hospitals, how would we know whether our results in treating patients with cystic fibrosis are as good as those obtained elsewhere?

Consider two similar colleges or universities, virtually equivalent in the degree to which they are selective and in the quality of their entering students, as well as in size, mission, finances, faculty composition, and facilities. Suppose campus A consistently outperforms campus B in terms of student learning on writing, critical thinking, and quantitative literacy goals as measured by independent panels judging student work samples. Presuming for the sake of argument that all other variables are equal, campus A clearly is performing better. What differences in institution A's culture, curricula, or pedagogy may account for such a difference? If campus A also outperforms campuses C, D, E, and others, it sets a benchmark for institutional performance.

Comparisons like these represent a form of benchmarking exemplified by the example of the treatment of cystic fibrosis in different hospitals. Such benchmarking—which, at its heart, depends on a process of learning from others—helps to impel improvement by raising aspirations and expectations. The usefulness and value of benchmarking depends, of course, on the care with which the criteria for excellence are established and on broad agreement among participants about those criteria and the means of measuring performance. These criteria become the standards, and measurements are standards based, not referenced to norms or constructed on curves. No two institutions of higher education are exactly alike, just as no two hospitals are; the characteristics of patients seen in one hospital will rarely be exactly the same as those of patients seen in another, and students attending one college will rarely be exactly like those who matriculated at a different institution. But it is possible to define a set of student and institutional parameters that are sufficiently similar among certain groups of schools to create a reasonable foundation for cross-institutional comparisons on certain key criteria for learning, just as it is possible to define such parameters for the treatment of cystic fibrosis, myocardial infarction, or stroke across the diversity of patients, regions, and hospitals.

At the institutional level, discovering that another college outperforms one's own campus on the fundamentals of student learning stimulates efforts to learn from their success and improve. At a far more microscopic but equally important level, the benchmarking process promotes student growth as well: confronted by superior work from peers similar to themselves, students may learn that greater effort, different study strategies, or more practice will enable them to reach greater achievement. We see this kind of benchmarking commonly in athletics (how else would college teams get to bowl games and postseason tournaments?) and performing arts (only the best performers get to Carnegie Hall), but it is just as applicable to the foundational aspects of college learning. Note how different true benchmarking is from the comparisons and rankings of institutions of higher education provided by magazines.

Endorsing benchmarking is far simpler than implementing it. Many leaders in higher education fear that cross-institutional comparisons will have invidious or damaging results: they doubt that faculties can reach agreement about the criteria and measurements, are concerned that identifying groups of similar institutions would be an impossible—or, worse, fraudulent—process, and question the ability of audiences outside higher education to understand and interpret the results. Similar objections greeted early attempts to benchmark treatment results for a variety of medical conditions and still obstruct the public disclosure of some comparative studies. But comparative benchmarking offers the possibility of documenting and inspiring excellence in higher learning.

Conclusion

Learning assessment in colleges and universities is perceived as an onerous task and is utilized sparingly as a means of enhancing instruction. Yet it is an essential way of making learning visible and providing an institution with data that can help better identify and remove barriers to higher learning among students. Providing appropriate and timely feedback to students and teachers during the process of learning, in a formative, diagnostic manner, offers students an appropriate and accurate sense of how well they are meeting learning objectives and allows time for remediation and reteaching. Moreover, such feedback signals and reinforces the faculty members' expected standards of achievement, allowing them to work with students toward a common goal.

When faculty members define high order learning objectives and create their assessments simultaneously, they are better able to eliminate the usual guessing game about what is expected and the universal question, "Will it be on the test?" In defining desired higher learning outcomes, we recognize that they are primarily collective and cumulative in nature and as such can best be taught and measured in a community of practice that more resembles an apprenticeship of learning than it does a shopping mall of individual boutique courses.

We need to develop cultures of assessment in higher education in which what constitutes expected learning and the criteria for excellence are clear to all participants. Ultimately, cross-institutional benchmarking of the quality and quantity of student learning offers the possibility of inspiring and achieving excellence in learning across the spectrum of colleges and universities. Fundamental to such a change in culture is radical change in the incentive and reward structures for faculty. Learning assessment as a form of teaching and learning must occur far more often, and this will require more effort on the part of faculty. Making one's expectations public, not to mention substantially raising expectations and standards beyond the norms today, requires far more time and effort on the part of both students and faculty. Unless the latter are duly rewarded for time spent on teaching for learning, and unless assessment is inextricably tied to that process, things will not change.

6

More Is Not Better, Better Is More

A Framework for Rethinking American Higher Education

Introduction

In this chapter we offer a framework for rethinking American under-graduate higher education, including the concepts, principles, models, and good practices we think constitute the foundation for a better system. The framework we suggest has its basis in both learning research, including the neurosciences, and our experience as educators, administrators, and consultants who have witnessed examples of excellence and helped colleges and universities begin the process of change for learning.

In our analysis, we explicitly reject the narrow focus on the costs and efficiency of higher education taken by critics who lament the absence in colleges and universities of a more corporate, or business-like, approach to mission and management. The unstated assumption behind this perspective—that there is nothing wrong with higher education that greater efficiency and lower costs will not remedy—is well intentioned, but myopic. We do *not* deny that most institutions of higher education could operate more efficiently, and we affirm that decreasing costs is important. But we assert three other points: first, that what is wrong with higher education in America today is more fundamental than its costs or levels of efficiency; second, that adopting a more businesslike operational model in colleges and universities would not alone solve those problems and might actually worsen them; and third, that the nature of the work done in higher education limits the applicability of technological and other innovations that have increased efficiency in other enterprises.

Proposals to change the usual and customary model of undergraduate education to permit students to complete baccalaureate degrees in three years[1] are a good example of interventions aimed at greater efficiency—a solution proposed as a way of reducing costs for students and their families, governments, and institutions themselves. This so-called reinvention of higher education might, or might not, increase efficiency (and, by the way, might, or might not, reduce costs). But it would certainly do further harm to the ability of colleges and universities to deliver *higher learning* as we have defined it in the first chapter of this book. We have no doubt that colleges could rush students through enough courses to allow them to accumulate a sufficient number of credits to graduate routinely in fewer than four years (or, worse, that colleges eager to recruit students into three-year programs could reduce the number of credits required for graduation), but we strongly believe there is more to higher learning than completing the required number of credits—not to mention the fact that there is more to college than courses. And what would happen to developmental learning, if all of it were squeezed into three years? To time on task? To reflection and meaning making? We can accelerate the construction of automobiles or robots, but nothing in learning research suggests that there is any wisdom to accelerating the emergence of a whole human being.[2]

Our real concern about higher education should be *value*, not efficiency. The question we should be asking is not "Does higher education cost too much?" Instead, we should ask the following:

- Does the quality and quantity of learning by students justify the cost?
- Are students leaving college prepared for the challenges of the twenty-first century?
- Will the public and society at large benefit from their investments in our institutions of higher education?

No amount of tuition, large or small, is worth it if students do not learn. Lower cost, and therefore lower tuition, do not automatically equal higher value—nor do higher cost and higher tuition. There is no reason in higher education today to believe that costs and quality are related in any linear way—if, in fact, they are related at all, beyond some threshold level of basic expenditures. Establishing social policy for higher education primarily on the basis of lowering costs makes no more sense than establishing health policy on that basis alone; we would not settle for cheaper health care if that left us with worse quality. Most analysts of our chronic crisis in health care would conclude, in fact, that we spend too much and get too little value—an argument we would make about American higher education today as well. In higher education as in health care, we should be seeking an approach that maximizes both quality and value across the board.

Higher education has experienced—and too often suffered from—any number of attempts to improve both productivity and efficiency. The most widespread of those practices is stretching instructional dollars by supplementing—or replacing—full-time faculty members (especially, full-time, tenure track faculty members) with part-time or adjunct faculty members (collectively referred to as contingent faculty). A purely economic analysis might suggest that this is a good idea: instead of paying higher salaries and benefits for full-time faculty, use part-time and adjunct faculty members to teach certain courses—especially classes for undergraduates in the first and second years, notably introductory and general education courses. (Never mind, for now, the troubling inherent assumption that undergraduates, general education, and introductory courses are somehow not worthy of the time and attention of members of the full-time, tenure-track, or tenured faculty). But an educational analysis exposes the flaws of this strategy: students who attend institutions that use part-time and adjunct faculty extensively often do not have substantial contact with full-time faculty during the critical first two years of college, when advising, mentoring, and the formation of trusted relationships with caring adults are especially important to both development and educational decision making. Depending to a large extent on part-time or adjunct faculty members could be compared to bringing in lower cost labor, independent from the rest of the project, to build the foundation when constructing a house; the regular workers don't particularly enjoy foundation work, nobody's going to see it, and after all, the paint job and roof are the most important and noticeable aspects, right? Most part-time and adjunct faculty members are paid—and typically, paid very poorly—only to teach specific courses; they are not compensated for advising, mentoring, or otherwise engaging with students outside the classroom. Less student-faculty engagement equals less persistence in school and lower rates of retention; a recent study of six institutions showed convincingly that "high levels of exposure to part-time faculty in the first year of college are consistently found to negatively affect student retention to the second year."[3] Common tactical decision? Yes. Cheaper? Perhaps, though a comprehensive analysis that includes the financial effects of dealing with lower retention (i.e., the costs of replacing students who leave) might show less benefit than some might claim. Better? No.

On the other hand, consider some examples of innovations that may improve quality—but take substantial amounts of educators' time, may not be especially efficient, and cannot be easily standardized, templated, or mass produced, if done well: first-year seminars, common reading experiences, comprehensive holistic advising, service learning, under-graduate research, cultural immersion experiences, and capstone courses. Achieving higher learning requires that students have many such experi-ences that demand individual attention, especially from full-time fac-ulty and staff—and therefore inherently reduce efficiency. There is no evidence whatsoever that systematically and unselectively shortening the time allowed for higher learning, or shorting the human resources invested in it, will do anything other than short circuit both quality and outcomes.

The great challenge of engaging most students in excellent learning experiences, like that of higher learning more generally, is one of scale. It is easy to find persuasive examples of particular programs that can be shown to improve learning for small groups of students (e.g., hon-ors programs or colleges); analyses of the success of those programs generally reveal that extensive engagement with faculty members was an important—and usually determinative—feature. All of these expe-riences, if well taught, can produce important milestones along the pathway of higher learning, from novice to master. All of them were conceived originally as small pilot projects and then mounted as larger demonstration projects: good, sound ideas awaiting generalization, dissemination, and wide implementation. But bringing them to scale would require substantial institutional change—placing, for example, higher priority on engagement with students among the criteria used to reward faculty members and ensuring that first-year undergraduates encounter full-time faculty members in their courses, from the freshman seminar to general education classes. Those changes would, in turn, require that learning be the first priority of the institution.

But what about technology? Can't computers fix this? Don't today's students do everything on their laptops, iPads, and smartphones anyway? Aren't computers the key to solving the scalability problem? Our progressive faith in the transformative ability of technology may mislead us here. Digital technologies have improved the efficiency, consistency, and reliability of so many processes—think of online shopping (or banking, or airline reservations), automated teller machines (ATMs), global positioning systems (GPS) for navigation, complex equipment that monitors multiple patient parameters in intensive care and surgery, and electronic highway toll payments (E-Z Pass and similar systems)—that we naturally assume they can do the same for higher education. But the promise of new technology in higher education, in terms of both lowering costs and improving quality, has not yet been, and we think will not be, borne out. The brain is not a machine, and, despite our ability to observe, measure, and explain its processes with increasing detail and sophistication, we should limit the enthusiasm with which we expect machines to add greater efficiency to those processes. Being able to look things up quickly on the Internet does not translate into being able to discern the value of information obtained there or to make constructive personal meaning of that information. Instant communication with someone from another culture, even if supported by a live, real-time video image of that person, does not constitute cultural immersion; when risk can be controlled as easily as clicking off the connection when someone or something online becomes challenging or uncomfortable, developmental education is not occurring. Research shows that most Americans selectively search for and read information on the Internet that reinforces their own points of view,[4] but one of the main goals of higher learning is to challenge students' existing, ingrained perspectives.

American optimism for technological solutions to our educational ills is not a new phenomenon. Our confidence in the probability that computer technology would greatly improve education led, in the 1980s and 1990s, to the fear that inequitable access to the tools of technological advancement would condemn some, or many, people to a modern form of enslavement. They would become unskilled "technopeasants"— members of society disadvantaged by their inability to use modern technology[5] and therefore condemned to menial employment. Educators voiced particular concern about students from less-wealthy K–12 school districts who might matriculate in college without the same computer skills as peers whose high schools had more resources and about the quality of learning for students in colleges that could not provide as many computers, or as much bandwidth, or as many information technology staff, as would be offered in more technology-rich institutions. Following the logic of those fears, educators worried that we would end up with new forms of inequity and discrimination based on different degrees of technological literacy.

Inequity and discrimination on various grounds remain serious limitations to our advancement as a civil and just society. But earlier concerns about the impact of differential levels of computer literacy among students in higher education have been themselves transformed into greater alarm about a more pressing problem: most students now enter college with reasonable levels of literacy and skill in information technology, but far too many leave without having acquired what we have defined as a transformative, higher education. In other words, we now have created technopeasants[6] of a completely different kind: people who have strong computer skills, including the ability to access an infinite yet always expanding universe of web-based information but who cannot generally make good or useful sense of all the material they find and collect—and who may not have developed sufficient ability to monitor and regulate their own use of the technologies available.

It would be hard to argue today, in any event, that the level of technological literacy among students otherwise qualified for admission to college is uniquely determined by the resources made available to them by K–12 schools, given the proliferation of computers, smartphones, tablets such as the iPad, and other information-handling devices in our society, and the rapid growth of Internet-based entertainment, communications, and networking tools. Computer games, played on various technology platforms, have become ubiquitous. Young Americans learn about technology from all of these sources and more, and in many venues that have nothing to do with their formal schooling. But knowing how to use social media and a variety of electronic gaming and communications devices and software does not translate into better preparedness for learning in college.[7] Debate continues, in fact, about the degree to which the use of information on the Internet dumbs down, rather than improves, learning, culture, and society[8]; obtaining information in small bites from websites of uncertain reliability may negatively affect the way we understand and make meaning. From the perspective of higher education, the burgeoning technologies that are transforming childhood and adolescence, changing communications styles, and causing both concern and new legislation about issues from Internet privacy to texting while driving have not made entering students better learners. More technology does not easily translate into or correlate with improvements in the outcomes of education.

Technology—good or bad, applied well or poorly, and distributed equitably or not—is neither the problem nor the solution. What is wrong, as suggested in earlier chapters, is that traditional age students now come to college *less* capable of taking advantage of a true college education—less emotionally ready, less prepared to read, write, and think critically, and with less of the resilience required to persevere in face of challenges. Moreover, larger and larger numbers of students matriculate with the burden of working while in school to pay for college—and, often, the responsibility of also supporting their families. The critical issue is not how we compress four years of college into three or how we better deploy computers in classrooms; it is that students start college unprepared for higher learning and that higher education has done little—and almost nothing, systematically—to offset students' antecedent deficits.

Our driving concerns must be quality and value, not cost and efficiency. But that does not mean that the solution to the problems of higher education today is just more money; throwing money indiscriminately at any of the problems we have identified is a step that betrays a lack of sufficient analysis and critical thought. Ultimately, rethinking higher education is not about figuring out how to offer more of what we have always done—more choices of academic programs (and types and sources of food), more luxurious residence halls, better climbing walls, more accessible and higher caliber technologies, and, of course, more parking. We assert, paradoxically, that more is not better—instead, better is more. In other words, just doing more of what we have already done will not get us out of the crisis that now faces higher education. Instead of doing more, we have to focus on quality and learning, which will mean doing things differently and better. And—this is equally paradoxical, in our increasingly technological world—becoming better in terms of the quality and quantity of student learning depends on increasing the handcrafted nature of higher education, rather than counting on shortcuts, technology, or other industrial approaches to improving efficiency.

Educational Excellence: A Handcrafted Apprenticeship

The core functional characteristics of the human brain and the ways in which we learn have not changed in the last many hundreds, or even thousands, of years. Techniques, methods, and formats of learning change, but the fundamentals of brain anatomy and function do not. We have observed the process of developmental learning as teachers, parents, employers, and psychologists; now, we can also observe that process as neuroscientists—but still, the process is the same.

Students once came to know other cultures primarily through novels and textbooks and then from films and slideshows; today, websites and immersion experiences, made possible by worldwide air travel and globalization in education, introduce them directly to innumerable people, places, and customs different from their own. But no matter how we observe it, and no matter the format in which it occurs, learning is learning—new experiences and knowledge stimulate structural and functional changes in the brain that we recognize behaviorally as change in the learner.

Humans learn best in a state of relaxed alertness and when they encounter both challenge and support—that is, when they are nurtured, but also when confronted with new ideas or experiences and held to high expectations. When we try to learn in an environment in which the elements of challenge and support are unbalanced, we do not learn as well. Too little support and our encounter with challenging material is more stressful than productive. Abundant support without parallel challenge—or the wrong kind of support, in which comfort without pressure of any kind is mistaken as a laudable goal—is as bad or worse: new material fails to inspire and motivate us. Excellence in learning is best achieved through the combination of hard work, perseverance, mentoring, and feedback from demanding and caring parents, teachers, professors, coaches, friends, and bosses. The true purpose of a college or university, then, is to create a rich and powerful learning environment that offers appropriate challenges, demanding teaching, supportive mentoring, and constructive feedback.

In this way, higher learning, as we understand it, is analogous to an apprenticeship, as we have suggested earlier—the intentional, progressive education of a novice, with eventual achievement of masterly competence. Such a process—regardless of the specific educational program or a student's intended career—requires personal and intellectual immersion in a carefully structured learning environment. In the initial, foundational stages of apprenticeship in higher learning, the student relies heavily on professors and advisors for initiating practice in the essential skills of thinking, acquiring and applying knowledge, and self-assessment—and for introducing and reinforcing the habits of mind, attitudes, dispositions, and behaviors that, when developed and reinforced over time, help one acquire and demonstrate the hallmarks of an educated person. The need for these introductions is why the first year in college is so critical to future student success. With each succeeding year, assuming that both teaching and learning are done well, should come greater competency. As they progress through college, students engaged in higher learning should gradually experience more intellectual independence and liberation, with expansion of knowledge, greater understanding, and, ultimately, perfection of the habits and skills that eventually permit full autonomy. The notion of a liberating education arises from both the goal of releasing the mind from the shackles of limited knowledge and narrow or untested perspectives and from the learner's progress toward self-directedness. Ultimately—again, if teaching and learning have been done well—students do and should become less reliant on the teachers of all kinds who have nurtured and challenged them.

The progressive growth of competency generates both autonomy and authority—along with qualities that scholars of higher education have referred to as savvy[9] or connoisseurship.[10] In his article on this topic, Kenneth Prewitt explains savvy as the ability to act on the basis of a shrewd understanding of the principles and structures that govern complex situations. "A savvy person," he says, "has those skills and insights that make for survival and success in what would otherwise be bewildering and intimidating situations"[11]—very valuable and desirable competencies in our complex, global twenty-first-century "flat world."[12] Prewitt defines multiple savvies: street savvy, the knowledge and sensitivity that separates outsiders from those in the know, the possession of which diminishes the threat one feels from chaos on the street; political savvy, in which a person is indoctrinated in the formal and informal rules, codes, and levers of power; entrepreneurial savvy, the know-how to make the intricacies of the marketplace work on behalf of one's new ideas and new products; and scientific savvy, which enables one to escape or avoid bewilderment or intimidation by the introduction of new technologies or scientific language. By definition, savvy citizens are not outsiders in their own society. "Rather than being manipulated [or feeling manipulated] by forces beyond understanding and beyond control, the citizen 'in-the-know' can make the system work," Prewitt further notes.[13] And, we would add, savvy citizens can initiate and facilitate change in the system itself.

Connoisseurship, which might be understood as a variation of savvy, is the superior knowledge that allows one to discriminate among what is most salient, most useful, and/or most relevant in a given field or topic; it is a sharpening of one's ability to appreciate differences, a kind of intellectual and observational virtuosity. Eisner writes, "Connoisseurship is the art of appreciation. It can be displayed in any realm in which the character, import, or value of objects, situations, and performances is distributed and variable."[14]

It requires that one be able to make use of a wide array of information and place experience in a wider context: "Where a connoisseur sees the differences, a novice sees the similarities."[15]

Virtuosity, connoisseurship, savvy—these are distinctive learning goals, different expressions of the development of expertise that cannot be realized through technology or achieved by the means and methods of mass production. They require the diligent and intentional application of hands-on techniques; they are handcrafted outcomes. Teachers, advisors, and mentors have essential, continuous, and indispensable roles in the achievement of these goals; they are the masters and guides in students' apprenticeships. The common antecedents of the development of any kind of expertise, however defined, are time, practice, challenge, and mentoring.

Immersion

What is required for novice apprentices to become masters? For someone who has little knowledge or experience in any area to become an expert? For an amateur to become a virtuoso, to gain savvy, to achieve connoisseurship? How can time, practice, challenge, and mentoring be woven together?

Immersion in the content and culture under study is important—probably essential. As Youngme Moon writes in her book *Different*, a treatise on marketing that emphasizes ways of differentiating one product among a large array of bewilderingly similar ones, "If every day were declared to be Halloween, it wouldn't be long before we would all be authorities on candy."[16] Going to a cooking school in France for ten weeks, spending a semester in Costa Rica or Sicily, interning in a legal firm, living in a foreign language theme house, doing an intensive undergraduate research project, participating in a full-time summer music performance camp, or going through basic training for the army are examples of immersion experiences—any of them qualitatively different from the far more casual learning modalities that are the norm on college and university campuses today, where, too often, less is less.

Consider, instead, an alternative. Imagine a college or university in which learning occurs through immersion in a powerful educational culture—a culture in which learning is an intentional preoccupation within and across courses, inside and outside the classroom. In that culture, learning how to think, solve problems, and write and speak well—and acquiring the expertise, virtuosity, savvy, and connoisseurship modeled by one's professors—are key elements of expected and standard practice. The emphasis is on *expected* and *standard* in that last sentence: that is, in a powerful educational culture, learning is a constant, intentional preoccupation for all students and all faculty—not just for a small, self-selected group of high performing students who make the institution work well for them or an even smaller group of dedicated professors whose values and commitments lead them to mentor, advise, challenge, and support students with or without the endorsement of colleagues and with or without recognition in promotion and tenure systems. In a powerful educational culture, teaching and learning are truly everybody's business—and that business is conducted day in and day out.

Apprenticeship in higher education requires sustained immersion in exactly that kind of powerful educational culture—what we will call a culture of serious teaching and learning. It requires that students take in the expectations, standards, norms, mores, beliefs, language, and moral dimensions of the community of teachers and learners that really compose the institution (as opposed to the troublesome, prevailing notion that an institution of higher education is its buildings and grounds, endowment, or athletic teams) for the purpose of promoting specific kinds of mastery. In an institution with such a culture, the intersecting behaviors of faculty, students, advisors, and staff occur within generally accepted norms that include consistently high expectations and standards and a collective acceptance of accountability. The campus of an institution that has created that kind of educational culture might feel distinctive even to a casual visitor; there would be a tone of seriousness about learning, ideas, and inquiry, manifest in obvious, comfortably informal conversations among students and faculty, strong attendance at performances and cultural events, and the availability of options other than large alcohol-fueled parties for evening and weekend entertainment. A culture of serious teaching and learning would intentionally create many occasions for transformational learning and encourage and expect students to take full advantage of those offerings. In such an institution, there would be a learning environment that purposefully pulled all members of the community upward. There would be no dumbing down in curriculum, courses, classes, or out-of-classroom learning experiences; rather, there would be a race to go higher and higher.

Note that while residential campuses with a dominant population of full-time undergraduates might have certain advantages in creating such a culture and learning environment, most of such campuses have not done so. Colleges and universities that have limited or no on-campus housing and/or provide educational programs for nontraditional and returning adult students can still foster the development of the qualities of culture and learning environment that support serious teaching and learning. From the perspective of educational quality, on-campus residency is not destiny; having students live on campus does not necessarily improve the learning environment and may weaken it. And the enrollment of part- or full-time nonresidential students with complex lives and commitments does not in and of itself prevent the members of a campus community from coming together as serious teachers and learners. Colleges and universities owe those students the same opportunities for engagement and the same high expectations and educational investments that they apply to full-time, traditional-age undergraduates.

Students immersed in a culture of serious teaching and learning would feel very challenged, but in the right ways. Occasions and situations that require the best of us, even when stressful, inspire us and elicit our best work and effort. We put in the time required; we work hard; we revise, revise, and revise again. Nothing in a serious educational culture suggests that we should do anything different—or anything less. But in a less demanding educational environment, students too often have the opportunity to do less, not more; to engage only a little, if at all; to sample, rather than immerse themselves in, disparate learning opportunities selected, as if choosing from restaurant menus. Still, they can reap gratifying returns: good grades, satisfactory numbers of accumulated credit hours, and, in the end, yes, degrees. Little challenge begets little effort; the path of least resistance is seductive . . . and normative. But given the opportunity, students can and will rise to the occasion. Confronted by the necessity of overcoming a learning challenge, well-prepared students perform admirably. The problem is that in modern higher education, they are seldom expected to do so.

One learning experience that reliably produces the conditions of immersion and creates the opportunity for transformation is study abroad—spending a quarter, semester, or more in another country. College students who do so often report that their time abroad was the most challenging and beneficial learning opportunity they experienced in college. Typically in overseas study, students necessarily and inevitably engage the unknown in a place far from home, without the usual, comfortable assumptions, structures, and systems of their native culture. They feel humbled and often thrown for a loop by their lack of familiarity and comfort with a foreign language and the customs, norms, and behaviors of people whose appearance, resources, and lives may differ markedly from their own. Students beginning study abroad therefore experience a condition of disequilibrium; cognitive psychologists call this destabilization, and it is a good thing, not a bad one. To cope, students' cognitive, emotional, and social antennae become sensitized to search for cues regarding appropriate cultural expectations and standards. Immersion thus produces disequilibrium, which catalyzes adaptation, which requires very focused attention and learning. Adaptation builds knowledge, but also appreciation, confidence, and pride. In an overseas immersion experience, one cannot avoid confronting difference—it is not possible to just walk away or turn off the computer. But by confronting difference head on and in person, one learns how rewarding overcoming such a challenge can be.

Two examples drawn from our own experiences come to mind. In the first, 15 students from a northeastern liberal arts college chose to spend a semester at Oxford University in England. Majoring mostly in English, history, comparative politics, and international economics, these students were intellectually bright, but seriously challenged by their new British peers, who had been originally accepted to study at Oxford. Visiting these students for an early morning breakfast three weeks after their term in England began, their own American college president asked them how things were going. They uniformly and enthusiastically claimed to be "loving it" and "learning so much." After breakfast, the students made a point of saying to their visitor, the president, that he could always catch them at Oxford's library when they were not in class. Having just recently built a very expensive new library and technology center on his own campus, which students visited infrequently outside of exam periods, the president asked why they were spending so much time in the Oxford library. "Well," one jumped in, "we have these tutorial sessions three times a week, in which 11 of us meet around a table with the tutor to discuss the assigned readings for the week. We are expected to participate and come prepared with two- or three-page papers." Another chimed in, "When you're on the line each class session, you spend a lot of time in the library getting ready."

Joyful yet skeptical, knowing all too well these students' usual behavior on their home campus, the president, playing the devil's advocate, asked, "I am a little confused. Back home we can barely get you to use our library, much less study and spend so much time reading and writing

for your classes, yet here you are saying you are enjoying this experience in which you are doing so much more work. What is going on?"
Two students, almost in unison, responded (in that somewhat mocking
tone of "Duh!"), "This is *Oxford*, and this is what they expect." Immersion, disequilibrium, and adaptation—in a culture of serious teaching
and learning.

The second example is from an American university in which 18 students, studying in a Muslim country, found their first several weeks to be
extremely disorienting, even though they had participated during a prior
semester in intensive language and cultural study. In classes and residences, for example, men and women were segregated and alcohol consumption was forbidden. With language and cultural immersion classes
for three hours each day, plus three additional courses, field trips, and
studying in the evenings, these students had virtually no free time. The
American professor in residence with them for the semester reported on
return the following about the trip:

> Early on our students were disoriented and extremely sensitive to their
> surroundings. They seemed constantly wary. Their usual outgoing, infor-
> mal behavior we see back home was muted and they quickly copied the
> dress and habits of their new peers. By the fourth week our students had
> made many new friends, were back to their more gregarious natures,
> and had adjusted well to their new surroundings. Yes, I heard the usual
> bitching and moaning about no alcohol, no dating, the lack of English
> language television, and the cold, unheated rooms at night, but their new-
> found diligence and willingness to play by a whole new set of rules seemed
> to belie deep concern in their complaints.

It is somewhat ironic, of course, that students find learning off campus in a foreign setting to be their most powerful college experience.
Upon reflection, however, this makes a great deal of sense. Learning
through immersion experiences requires intense engagement; with
greater engagement comes heightened awareness, increased energy, and a
kind of integrated cognitive and emotional commitment. Students commonly report afterward "losing myself in the moment" and say that time
flew by. These experiences are challenging and often stressful; but leaving, while clearly an option in many cases, is so counter normative that
students find ways to adapt. Responding to questions about how they
adapted to an environment, culture, and expectations so different from

their usual ones, students may start by saying it was sink or swim—and any experience described that way tends to focus the mind—yet almost always conclude saying, "I wouldn't trade it for anything."

For students to achieve the goals of higher learning, we need to create campus cultures that approximate similarly demanding immersion environments. Some instructive models, and microcultures, are commonplace on campuses. Consider the following as examples: fraternities and sororities, athletic teams, honors programs and colleges, learning communities, themed residences (e.g., focused on languages, community service, art and music, sustainability), and certain clusters of students who share both employment and educational or programming responsibilities (e.g., resident assistants, peer educators, orientation guides). In some institutions, one could add certain student organizations (especially preprofessional and service groups). In many colleges and universities, demanding and revered professors create their own islands of cultural immersion in learning. Some of these microcultures are more intense than others; they differ in the nobility of their purposes (and their actions), the degree of their commitment to learning, and the success they can claim. But they share many of the features of learning by immersion, for good or ill. Few pledges who are initiated into social fraternities would describe the process as anything other than a challenging immersion experience; they would describe the stress of having to learn a new language, adapt to new cultural norms, and meet specific group expectations. Students who choose to reside in learning communities would probably describe a far less intense experience, but would nonetheless note the impact of becoming a member of a new community and adapting to its culture.

The challenge is to construct, on each campus and across the diversity of institutional types and student demographics, an institutionwide culture of serious teaching and learning that provides an integrated and purposeful educational experience in which students intentionally immerse themselves. Attending college would be conceived as entering the unknown, traveling to a foreign land in which students encounter different expectations and standards, receive both challenge and support, and are invited to participate in a set of transformative learning experiences that will literally change their lives. Entering such a cultural exchange, as it were, students would have to understand the essential reciprocity necessary to participate: there would be a clear social contract, the provisions of which would hold students responsible for bringing a willingness to work hard, in return for which professors would mentor them in the skills, temperament, knowledge, and collective wisdom of higher learning. A few, and sometimes many, microcultures of high expectations and achievement exist on most campuses, but, by definition, those cultures are micro, not macro. It is the need to change the larger institutional culture that demands change for learning.

Change the Culture, Change the Outcomes

As consultants, we often hear faculty members speak of a kind of academic predeterminism: "If you want better outcomes, admit better students!" Challenging the idea that anything in institutional—or, especially, faculty—culture needs to change, professors often decry students' lack of preparedness for college, complain about the small amounts of effort students seem willing to invest in their courses, express irritation at the poor quality of students' papers and class presentations, and talk about how frustrated they are with the administration (a nameless, faceless, personification of institutional bureaucracy) and its priorities (or low standards) in admissions and enrollment management. A strange implication of these arguments is that college itself is powerless to change students—that students are who, and what, they are, and they will, or won't, succeed—or that college can only change high-performing, well-qualified, academically superior students. Were that true, then the only logical answer would indeed be to admit better students.

But we know that the claim of academic predeterminism is a cop-out. Certainly students have different levels of preparedness, intellectual capacity, cognitive flexibility, earnestness, and motivation; across any population of students, there are various frequencies of cognitive challenges, from attention deficit disorder to distraction related to personal or family problems. Ignoring that spectrum and focusing only on the high-end students, colleges could make themselves selective enough that they admitted only students who will succeed no matter what the institution does or does not do; that is, they could enroll only students who are so capable and motivated that they will support and retain themselves, as it were. And those students would, of course, attract the attention and interest of faculty members, who would find mentoring them to be a great pleasure. The responsibility and mission of higher education, however, is not so simple as escorting superbly qualified students through necessary classes and on to graduation. And there is strong evidence that students with a spectrum of qualifications and backgrounds can succeed given the influence of a strong culture of teaching and learning.

Among children and adolescents in our primary and secondary schools, socioeconomic status (SES) is a powerful—albeit not the only—predictor of educational achievement.[17] Students who come from homes in which they were well fed, whose parents read to them early and often in childhood, who had appropriate health care, and who had easy access to libraries and museums, learn better. SES is a surrogate marker for those advantages; families with less income are less likely to have a variety of healthy and attractive foods, parents at home with time for reading, and access to health care and cultural events and resources. Higher SES then represents the amalgamation of social, economic, and cultural capital that creates substantial advantages in preparation for and during schooling at all levels. But SES—low or high—is not the only determinant of college outcomes. (Any reader can probably recall examples of notable exceptions to the expected rule—students from privileged families who failed to learn and students from truly desperate financial and social conditions who excelled.) The impact of SES can be modified or overcome by an educational culture that helps students compensate for the consequences of a lack of financial resources. One has only to look at those islands of exceptionally successful urban schools surrounded by a large sea of failing ones; in every case, there are differences in educational culture.

A recent study found that children growing up in homes with many books go on to at least three more years of schooling than children from bookless homes—an outcome that was independent of the nation in which the study was conducted, as well as parents' education, occupation, and social and economic class.[18] This research, conducted in 27 nations, attributes the quantitative relationship of books at home to persistence in school as evidence of a scholarly culture that creates advantages for children and does so more than having university-educated or professional parents. Furthermore, the findings held equally well in rich nations as in poor ones and in nations with vastly different economic, political, and social structures. The authors summarize that "we find that parents' commitment to scholarly culture, manifest by a large home library, greatly enhances their children's educational attainment . . . scholarly culture provides skills and knowledge that are central to literacy and numeracy."[19] This cultural evidence gets to the heart of matter: the quality of learning environments has more influence than many other factors in determining educational outcomes.

Four Scenarios: Learning Cultures

What kinds of learning cultures do we believe are most effective? Consider the following four scenarios and decide which one(s) you would be willing to support with your tuition payments, taxes, or philanthropic dollars. To which institution would you prefer to send your son or daughter?

The scenarios represent four different undergraduate models along a continuum of American college and university programs. Each is the operational expression of an institution's mission statement, demonstrating how the institution accomplishes what it promises—which is to provide the best higher education possible.

1. Classic College

Classic College prides itself on its return to essential education for the twenty-first century and has constructed a four-year curriculum centered on the "great works." Classic College believes that the great works include not only great texts associated with history, social science, humanities, fine arts, and the sciences, but also exceptional works of art, musical compositions, movies, videos, and so on; the college also recognizes and incorporates other great works from nonwestern intellectual and artistic traditions. The faculty members of the college have come together and agreed to teach 32 courses that all undergraduates are required to take and pass. They have also agreed to read all of the required texts within the first year of being hired and to team teach in each other's classes as often as possible. Faculty members are the only student advisors, and monthly advising meetings are mandatory.

The pedagogy is British tutorial style, using the Socratic method. Nine to 11 students meet five days per week with a professor to discuss required texts and make oral presentations of their own written analysis of the text material. Each class requires a final paper, each year ends with a comprehensive exam, and a senior thesis in the final year with an oral defense is required of all students. Faculty members' expectations are high and grading is quite rigorous. Classic College attracts a highly motivated group of students who have generally found their high school experiences unchallenging.

2. All-American University

All-American University prides itself on representing the best of twenty-first century American higher education. It has adopted the popular stance of many American colleges and universities by offering a combination of liberal education through its general education requirements and professional education through its majors in arts and sciences and its professional schools—business, education, journalism, engineering, and pharmacy.

General education at All-American begins with a required first-year seminar that helps orient students to college. Each of the 135 sections is taught by different faculty members (usually, in practice, by adjuncts or graduate students). Instructors choose their own books, reading lists, and themes for their section. The remainder of the general education curriculum requires students to choose three courses in the social sciences, three in humanities, one in fine arts, two in the sciences, one in math, and one that satisfies a diversity requirement.

The All-American curriculum is based on the faculty's belief that students are best treated as customers or consumers who have (or whose parents have) spent a lot of money on tuition and should therefore be allowed a maximum of free choice in building their course schedule. Indeed, students are permitted to go to any classes they wish during the first week of each term (known as the shopping period), at the end of which they can drop the courses they no longer wish to take. Class sizes range from eight to 125 with a mode of 27.

Expectations for students and standards in each course vary, but 73 percent of students achieve grade point averages of B or better. Students are often graded on a curve and are required to do little writing; they average less than 13 hours per week of homework, exactly at the national higher education average. Midterms and finals are the usual forms of assessment and capstone courses in the senior year are the prerogative of each department. All-American University attracts reasonably able students who have achieved moderately high SAT/ACT scores and B+ or better high school averages, typically along with a long list of cocurricular and community service activities.

3. Red, White, and Blue University

Red, White, and Blue University is referred to as Ivy League. It is a major comprehensive research university with many National Academy of Sciences members on the faculty. It is ranked among the top 25 American universities for research expertise and funding, and it accepts only 12 percent of applicants, who rank in the top 2 percent of all high school graduates in the country. Faculty members are hired and retained for their scholarly and research prowess and are primarily focused on their graduate students. Faculty members at Red, White, and Blue believe that their highly motivated, well-qualified students are quite capable of knowing what is good for themselves and equipped with the capability of designing their own course of study; thus there are no required courses in the general education curriculum. The presumption is that through good advising, students will select optimal educational programming.

All students have assigned faculty advisors, and they have the additional option of getting advising through the universitywide advising center staffed by professional advisors. Most opt for the advising center when they need schedules approved because faculty members keep minimal office hours. Students are promised the opportunity to work with faculty on research projects, but, in reality, only 17 percent of undergraduates are actually afforded that opportunity. Students vary in their effort, with many designing their own major; 83 percent graduated last year with honors.

4. Connoisseur University

Connoisseur University (CU) is a private, urban university serving approximately five thousand students. Over the past decade, CU has totally revamped its undergraduate program. The reinvented undergraduate experience now includes the following key attributes: (1) faculty agreement on an extensive, required core curriculum that spans the four undergraduate years, beginning with first-year seminars; (2) eight common required core courses across the disciplines; (3) extensive and intensive reading and writing requirements across the curriculum, including general education comprehensive exams and mandatory writing portfolios assessed by faculty panels at the end of the sophomore year; (4) undergraduate research projects in concert with faculty advisors during the junior year; and (5) capstone courses and theses required during the senior year.

The entire curriculum, institutional expectations, and standards of excellence are published on the institution's website as part of its admissions narrative. The website also includes examples of student work throughout the four years, including senior capstone theses and undergraduate research projects. Students are assigned faculty advisors/mentors when they are admitted, and, upon choosing a major, a second faculty advisor is assigned. Finally, a culture of assessment has been created through which students are provided constant feedback, with and without grades, within and across courses, as a way to signal faculty expectations and standards and to offer formative feedback during learning, when there is still an opportunity for students and professors to make changes.

Students are assigned to learning communities in much the same way law students often create such study groups. During the next decade, Connoisseur University plans to create a residential college structure emulating those in practice at Harvard and Yale to institutionalize the learning community concept.

Key Principles: A Culture of Higher Learning

Many of us might want to send our college-bound children to Connoisseur University. But each of the four scenarios contains a few or many of the attributes of a productive culture of learning; they illustrate not only common flaws in higher education today, but also the application of certain key principles that support transformative higher learning—learning that is developmental, intentional, holistic, cumulative and collective, coherent and integrated, challenging and demanding, and supported by distinctive institutional values, assumptions, expectations, and practices.

With the concepts discussed earlier and these examples in mind, we can identify ten fundamental principles that are useful benchmarks in creating an institutional culture of serious teaching and learning in higher education. We offer them as a package, or constellation, of principles that, *when practiced together and applied intentionally and rigorously*, make a significant difference in the quality and quantity of learning and thereby promise a greater educational bang for the buck. Although we recognize that the list, taken in its entirely, may at first seem intimidating and cost-prohibitive, we do *not* mean to suggest that the piecemeal adoption of one or a few of these principles will make a sustained difference.

Having reviewed the ten core principles, we will then offer examples of curricula and pedagogy that logically flow from them in making up the characteristics of a college or university that intentionally supports student learning and success.

The first principle speaks of institutional mission and purposes; the next three, of the nature of learning itself, and the final six of the distinctive elements of a learning-centered institutional culture.

1. Intentional Emphasis on Learning

Providing the opportunity for transformative higher learning demands the intentional creation and coordination of outstanding teaching and research, enriched educational experiences, and rewarding campus life. Transformative learning cannot be left to chance. Intentional efforts to promote transformative learning always require institutional change; the status quo in most institutions does not meet expectations and will not support the kind of enriched educational experiences that a college or university focused on learning wishes to provide.

An emphasis on learning represents a critical and foundational paradigm shift—from an instructional orientation focused on professors to a learning orientation focused on students.[20] Unfortunately, institutional change among colleges and universities is commonly impelled by economics and is rarely focused on student learning. When there is such a focus on learning, however, priority setting, budgeting, changes in programs, hiring, curriculum, incentive and reward systems, and institutional assessment are all judged by their contributions to improving learning. Improving learning becomes the primary purpose for change at all levels, with everything else understood as means to that end. This is the key principle of *change for learning*. In the next chapter, we will discuss how institutions can make learning their touchstone for decision making.

2. Holistic Learning

The nature of learning is holistic: intellectual development is inextricably connected to psychological, emotional, social, civic, and physical development. Student development, in the sense of progressive personal and psychosocial maturation, is interwoven with the acquisition, integration, and application of knowledge; the whole of it is learning (see Chapters 3 and 4 for a complete explication of this point). Learning thus includes identity formation as well as the development of resilience, perseverance, and emotional maturity. This holistic notion of higher education challenges the usual faculty conception of learning as mostly cognitive and/or classroom and credit-hour based. The nature of holistic learning requires that students become active, engaged learners in and out of class. The intentional interaction of theory and practice must be built into undergraduate curriculum and pedagogy. Problem solving and inquiry become important learning modalities. Formative assessment and frequent feedback are important parts of teaching and learning wherever they occur, and the academic and student affairs divisions of the institution must work together to promote student learning and success. Questions of the primacy of academic affairs or the independence of student affairs become less important than the principle of collaboration in the interest of supporting holistic learning.

3. Cumulative and Collective Learning

As discussed in Chapter 5, the core outcomes proffered by higher education (e.g., critical thinking; analytical reasoning; ethical development; quantitative reasoning; effective written and oral communication; the ability to use knowledge to solve problems, imagine solutions, and ask important questions; and the mastery of professional expertise) are not and cannot be learned in any one or a few required courses or out-of-classroom learning experiences. Such learning requires practice and feedback, through literally hundreds of opportunities that must be intentionally required, planned, provided, and assessed. One or two required writing courses, for example, do not produce competent writers; the presidency of one student organization does not a leader make, and the ability to take the perspective of others does not emerge after a single classroom exercise or workshop on diversity. The core higher education outcomes are necessarily learned cumulatively and collectively, throughout the entire undergraduate program, and thus are the shared responsibility of the entire faculty and staff. Good teaching and advising must take account of all of the ways and places in which learning occurs and incorporate a progressive, cumulative perspective in designing students' educational programs.

4. Coherent and Integrated Learning

Higher learning is not just information piled higher and higher, but knowledge that has been structured and integrated by students into learning that is personally meaningful, informs authentic problem solving, inspires imagination, and enables further learning. Knowledge acquired in various contexts and courses must somehow be knit together to form a coherent, integrated whole; ways of thinking and understanding developed in one course or in a sequence of learning experiences must be made transferable and applicable to others. Coherence and integration demand the creation of intentional links among in-class and out-of-class learning as well. Intentional learning experiences in residences, athletic teams, clubs and organizations, and civic activities, for example, contribute to net learning and can inform, extend, and enhance learning in courses and classrooms. It is the role of educators, including advisors, to help students discern the connections among all learning experiences. Research in the factors that support student success and the scholarship of teaching and learning clearly demonstrate the importance of tight coupling—intentionally linking learning experiences in and out of the classroom, across general education and majors, and through all years in school.

5. Challenging and Rigorous Curriculum:
High Public Expectations and Standards

Most research suggests that institutions with higher expectations and standards for students' work offer their students a greater quality and quantity of learning. Transformative learning is catalyzed by challenge. Such challenge requires that educators have high expectations for students—and for themselves as teachers—by demanding rigorous reading, writing, critical thinking, and problem solving. This insistence on rigor is signaled and reinforced by high expectations, substantial standards, authentic assessment, and timely and appropriate feedback. Similarly high standards and expectations of rigor must apply to both in-class and out-of-classroom learning experiences.

6. Academic Engaged Time

Not surprisingly, research has found that the more time students spend actively engaged in their studies, the more and better they learn. But simply being busy, as most students are, is not sufficient. Rather, the greatest impact on the quality and quantity of learning is produced by sufficient amounts of appropriately engaged time, such as intentional reflection, reading, writing, meeting with faculty members, conducting research, and immersing oneself in another culture. In this scenario, student effort outside of class would range from 25 to 40 hours per week—rather than the current average of 10 to 13 hours in colleges and universities in the United States.[21]

7. Engagement of Students with Full-Time Faculty

In an institution with a serious educational culture and a commitment to transformative learning and student success, teaching and learning are never contingent; they are, in fact, the *sine qua non* of mission, purposes, priorities, and the student experience. To ensure student learning of high quality and quantity, colleges and universities are obligated to provide the highest quality faculty possible *for all students*—not just for graduate students or upper division undergraduate majors. Of all the places in which an institution might skimp on expenses to save money, the quality of the faculty should be the least. Nothing is more important; the faculty is the institution. Presidents and other administrators come and go, but the intellectual capital—the most precious asset—of the institution is, always has been, and always will be, the faculty; members of the faculty are the sole resource without which no college or university can succeed. Students have the best undergraduate experience and the greatest degrees of educational achievement when they can regularly, predictably, and consistently engage with full-time faculty members who have a long-term commitment to the institution and its mission and values. Questions of the importance and essentiality of tenure continue to be debated in and out of higher education, but there is no question that there is no substitute for dedicated, demanding, caring faculty members who teach, advise, mentor, guide, and support students.

Although we think of a full-time faculty member in one particular way—a tenure-track professor who is accountable for achieving goals in all three traditional areas of faculty work (teaching, research and scholarship, and service)—some colleges and universities have begun to introduce variations in this standard conception. Professional schools, especially in the health sciences, have long recognized that they cannot expect every full-time faculty member to be a "triple threat," excelling in all three areas. Accordingly, they have developed alternative tracks for full-time faculty that may lead to tenure or long-term contracts; in addition to professors with the full range of traditional responsibilities, there are now research professors and clinical professors (sometimes called clinician educators). Some universities have now introduced variants of those models in nonprofessional academic programs, permitting selected full-time faculty members to have primarily teaching roles, usually with modifications in their titles (e.g., assistant teaching professor). These arrangements solve two of the problems of dependency on contingent faculty—full-time teaching faculty are not contingent, and they are expected to engage with and advise students—but introduce other concerns, such as the perceived comparative value or credibility of a teaching professor versus a traditional tenure-track professor. Many faculty members and academic administrators oppose these alternative models because they recognize and celebrate the inherent value of linking teaching, research and scholarship, and service in the work of professors. But the presumption that a good researcher makes a better teacher is unproven, and many "triple threat" professors find that the components of their roles are competitive more than they are complementary.

Unfortunately, the key requirement described earlier (dedicated, demanding, caring faculty members who teach, advise, mentor, guide, and support students) is not recognized—or, at least, not applied—on many campuses. The U.S. Department of Education's reports on the characteristics of employees in postsecondary institutions show that the proportion of college instructors who are tenured, or even on the tenure track, dropped from 57 percent in 1975 to 31 percent in 2007; that percentage likely continues to drop, and, overall, only about a quarter of the teachers who today's students encounter in college classrooms have any kind of tenure status in the institution.[22] Contingent faculty members—the part-time and adjunct teachers who provide most of the instruction to many undergraduates—typically do not have the same resources (offices, equipment, technology, etc.), access to professional development for improving their teaching, or, most important, *time* to work with students outside the classroom. We do not question the dedication of many contingent faculty members to their work or to the students they teach. But in the word contingent itself is the weakness of the model in which they are employed: temporary, year-to-year employment does not foster any sense of permanence, bonding, or connection to the institution—all qualities that promote effectiveness among faculty members engaged with students in higher learning.

8. Advising/Mentoring as Teaching

Research shows that advising, done well, can be a significant, positive factor in retention and student success. Students deeply value and need a trusted human relationship, especially with one or more members of the faculty (whom they most admire and respect). Especially in the first two years of college, students require significant advising—meaning advising through which they not only receive timely and accurate information to make sense of what seems to be confusing and contradictory, but also to experience challenge and support through discussions in which they are questioned about their aspirations (or lack thereof) and are supported and affirmed by caring adults. Access to such advice and wisdom is crucial when one is learning to navigate a plethora of new opportunities and requirements; it is all the more important given students' inevitable encounter with myriad existential questions—What is worth pursuing? Why is this course or program useful to me in the future? Should I consider business, medicine, law, or teaching? Such advising is a core, central element of the apprenticeship model; advisors provide critical assistance as students grow from novice to expert competency.

9. Assessment as Teaching and Learning

During the past decade, discussions about the assessment of student learning have centered mostly on demands for external accountability—demands that are resisted by many professors and administrators for reasons that are both sound and flawed. But assessment utilized formatively, as a teaching and learning tool during instruction to provide timely and productive feedback to students, has three important benefits: (1) it signals the expectations and standards of faculty and the institution, (2) it helps students learn how to judge their own work, and (3) it provides meaningful data that help educators improve learning experiences. Good advising—which is, likewise, a process of teaching and learning—should also include explicit goals and clearly articulated desired outcomes; assessment of the achievement of those goals and outcomes provides critical information that allows advisors to improve their performance and strengthen the positive impact of advising on students' educational experience. Assessment seen primarily as a summative tool for grading certainly has its own legitimate place in higher education, but it is not in and of itself a potent method of generating and using data for supporting learning and improving teaching. Part of a culture of serious teaching and learning is the infusion of assessment in educational programming at all levels.

10. General Education as Introduction to the "Great Conversation"

General education, at its best, introduces students to a universe of ideas, perspectives, and ways of knowing not encountered in high school, and it catalyzes the passionate pursuit of study in a major. Educators often think of general education as the doorway to the "great conversation"—the continuing, ages-old discussion among liberally educated human beings about the large, overarching questions of life itself—Who are we? Why are we here? What does it mean to be human? What is our relationship to nature, the universe, the past, and the future? What matters? General education is not meant to be, as most students experience it, courses to get out of the way so one can get to the the major—the learning that really counts. Naively believing that choice and/or giving customers what they want are educationally appropriate or viable pathways, many institutions ask students to meet distribution requirements—one from Humanities column A, one from Science column B, for example—rather than requiring that all students complete a designated set of courses that compose the core curriculum—which is, as it should be, an expression of what the collective faculty believes all students should learn, regardless of their eventual choice of major and career. Faculties have that responsibility—to come together and agree on what is important for their students to learn and to communicate what is important, and why it is so, to students. After all, not all learning or choices are equal in value. Faculty must articulate a clear notion of the cultural literacy worthy of a liberating education.[23]

Outline of a Distinguished Program of Liberal Education in a Culture of Higher Learning

What would a real undergraduate education program look like, in action, informed by these principles? When applied in practice, how do these principles create curriculum and pedagogy? What would students experience in a culture of serious teaching and learning? How would an institution that changed for learning actually work, day to day? In the following paragraphs we offer an outline of eight attributes that, when taken together, can create a demanding but supportive environment that immerses students in the serious work of learning. Educators might recognize some—but not all—of these components as characteristics of existing educational programs at their own institution. We laud every effort to take these individual steps, yet again must affirm that in the absence of every piece of the puzzle, students may miss out on a critical element in their holistic, cumulative, transformative education. It is the synchronous coordination of all of these efforts that drives students toward the achievement of higher learning.

Required, Common New Student Orientation and First-Year Seminars

College, as we imagine it, should be understood as both an apprenticeship in higher learning and an immersion experience in a new culture; as is true for any immersion experience, a thorough orientation to the people, language, customs, relationships, expectations, and standards of the new culture is indispensable for successful adaptation and socialization. In other words, starting college should be seen as a process of acculturation, requiring thoughtfully designed and delivered orientation programs that both explicate the features and expectations of the new culture and provide support as students move through disequilibrium into accommodation.

Orientation should start during the summer, before classes begin, and continue during the period of transition onto campus; it should include a common summer reading experience (in which new students all read, and come to campus prepared to discuss, a book selected by the faculty). Many faculty members are distressed by the degree to which orientation programs on their campuses have become entertainment-centered, socially oriented experiences in which there is little intellectual focus; a good orientation program should not only acknowledge but emphasize the mind and focus on how students will learn. This is not to say that orientation should not also include the kind of information that travelers to a new place always need—where things are, what services are available, how to use them, what the institution's systems and pathways are, and so on. But an orientation program that neglects or marginalizes thinking and learning—or one that substitutes playful ice breakers for true, spirited community building—does no justice to the purpose and mission of higher education. Colleges are educational institutions, not summer camps.

Following orientation, students should begin a yearlong first-year experience program—best conceived and implemented as small group seminars led by full-time faculty members. Through that year, students would gain valuable experience, get to know faculty members, and gather firsthand information about standards and expectations; the presence of full-time faculty, including senior professors, in first-year seminars signals the faculty's seriousness about setting and communicating high expectations and promoting readiness for college work.

Although faculty leadership in the first-year seminars is important, the seminars can be collaboratively team taught by faculty and professional staff (especially from student affairs) to introduce students to different ways of thinking, knowing, and teaching and to expose them to conflicting ideas and perspectives. Good first-year seminars include significant reading, writing, and oral presentations. The specific content can be chosen by the individual teaching professors, as long as all professors responsible for first-year seminars collectively agree on the overall desired learning outcomes for the experience. Seminars focused on, as examples, the debate about global warming, the influence of slavery on the development of jazz, the decline of print media in the age of the Internet, poetry inspired by the epidemic of AIDS, or the factors leading to the financial and economic crisis of 2007 can each, in their own ways, introduce students to the importance of and demand for critical thinking, the need for intense preparation and effort, the value of close reading, and the sharing of common content and language.

Furthermore, such seminars help to create community—certainly among students in the seminars, but also among the faculty and staff members who teach them—and introduce students to the concepts of continuous learning assessment and feedback. The seminar functions as a kind of microculture that illustrates and explains the characteristics of the greater culture of teaching and learning of which it is a critical part. These first-year courses therefore should be considered by the faculty as vitally important because they serve as an exceptional introduction to the institution's core curriculum and, ultimately, to the work of the disciplines in the majors.

Close Advising and Mentoring

In most American colleges and universities, student advising does not consistently meet desired goals for students, faculty, or staff. Advising is too often narrowly understood by students and faculty alike as an administrative burden, primarily an exercise in meeting academic program requirements and overcoming the challenges of scheduling. In complex university environments, where students must choose among a vast and constantly changing array of programs and courses, advising devolves into a coping strategy at best. A premium is typically placed on the transfer of information, whereby students are expected to engage with the institution's website to find lists of program requirements and available courses. Meetings with the professional advising staff—and, typically, with faculty advisors—are occasional, hurried, focused on locating or justifying exceptions to various rules, and usually dissatisfying for all concerned. Given the purpose of higher education, however, this narrow conception of advising as merely information management is as inadequate a model for advising as it is for teaching.

Paradoxically, there is general agreement among faculty and staff in most institutions that advising is a core responsibility and a key element for student success, even while it is, in actual practice, uncoordinated, poorly organized, inefficient, implemented with inadequate resources by faculty or staff who feel insufficiently prepared, and widely acknowledged to be ineffective. It is, then, no wonder that advising and its results are commonly sources of great frustration for students and faculty alike. The prevalence, severity, and effects of psychological and emotional problems experienced by students have created anxiety among advisors regarding their preparedness to work with students who are extraordinary persons, as opposed to ordinary persons facing extraordinary pressures.

Advising at its best is a powerful form of teaching and learning. Broadly defined, good advising embraces not only information sharing among faculty, staff, and students (developing and organizing the student's academic program, ensuring compliance with requirements, choosing and sequencing courses), but also advice and assistance from personal and academic support units including financial aid, career services, disabled student services, health and counseling services, and study abroad programs. The creation of a more coherent, robust, and coordinated advising system is among the most important interventions any college can implement to promote the achievement of desired student learning outcomes—and it is, as noted earlier, a key element of the apprenticeship model.

Advising should make clear the links among courses, between general education and the majors and between in- and out-of-classroom learning experiences. Similarly, good advising should help students recognize the relationships among, and integrate the conclusions reached in, all personal and academic support services. In these ways, advising, when done well, reduces the fragmentation of the educational experience and, in the process, reduces uncertainty and anxiety. In those and other ways, good advising promotes the development of expertise.

Colleges and universities can preserve necessary diversity in the content and format of advising while seeking to establish a common philosophy regarding student service, service standards and assessment tools, technology support, and professional development processes and resources. The object would be to strengthen and support excellence in advising, including advising by faculty members—but not to demand uniformity, undermine faculty autonomy, or displace faculty members from their essential roles as trusted academic advisors. Within the larger framework of advising to support transformative learning, there is a need for a specific approach to first-year student advising that engages students during recruitment, admission, orientation, and the first year; this plan may include connecting the first-year seminars to an advising function and requiring specific advising protocols during the first year.

Today, institutions need to differentiate the kind and intensity of advising provided for different students at different times, aligned with the sequence of student learning and progress. It is especially important to be able to provide more intense advising to students when they have more significant needs—including the development of surveillance and early alert systems to detect signs of academic or personal distress and case management for students with complex and intersecting challenges or needs. Levels of service should be aligned with (1) the complexity of the questions being addressed and (2) students' needs and personal and cultural characteristics.

Core Curriculum

A core curriculum forces members of the faculty to reach consensus about what it is they, as a collective, expect students to learn in college—that is, what the desired learning outcomes for all undergraduates are, regardless of their selection of majors. Designing a core curriculum requires that the faculty members have a collective notion of what cultural literacy means to them, demands that faculty members from different disciplines come together to integrate content (and, often, to teach with one another), sends a clear and unmistakable message to students about what learning is most important, promotes the creation of a common foundation of knowledge and cognitive skills that can be expected of every graduate, and increases the chances that students will experience coherence as they look for connections and linkages among the things they are learning and the learning experiences in which they engage. Furthermore, a core curriculum is a potentially powerful tool to articulate rigorous expectations and standards, and thus it can help make clear to students what is meant by the institution's educational mission as realized in a culture of serious teaching and learning. While the specific choices of content will vary, a core curriculum should always include study of the humanities, arts, social sciences, natural sciences, and mathematics (broadly defined: if the goal is quantitative literacy, it might be achieved through an applied mathematics course in statistics). A broad portfolio of courses from all of these areas creates the conditions in which students who might not have considered majoring in some particular area—often, in mathematics or the natural sciences, disciplines for which the barriers to entry are perceived to be relatively high—begin to consider those disciplines as realistic options. The presence of mathematics and natural sciences courses as requirements in the general education curriculum also tells prospective students that the institution is demanding and rigorous, since students (and parents) often associate courses in those disciplines (rightly or wrongly) with greater challenge.

Courses that are part of the core curriculum might well be interdisciplinary, given the intersecting complexity of knowledge today; interdisciplinary courses have the advantage of drawing upon different but complementary faculty expertise, and, if well planned and delivered, do not undermine the authority and value of the disciplines themselves. (A recognized danger in the casual construction of interdisciplinary courses is the risk of their becoming watered down or unfocused to the point that they are nondisciplinary, or even counterdisciplinary, rather than interdisciplinary.) One particularly successful application of an interdisciplinary approach has been in natural science courses; some institutions have approached the required general education science course as an introduction not only to basic content in biology, chemistry, and physics, but also to science as a way of knowing and understanding the world and its phenomena. This approach is far superior to the fabled physics for poets courses developed in some colleges to provide an easy out for students who had no interest in science or mathematics, instead of forcing timid undergraduates to actually learn something serious about science and the scientific method.

Writing, Critical Thinking, Problem Solving, and Ethical/ Moral Development Across the Curriculum

These broad learning outcomes—each of them deeply fundamental to a transformative liberal education and each of them important to all future employers of all students—cannot be mastered in any one or a few learning experiences. While specific courses, especially in general education, may focus sharply on writing, ultimately the achievement of desired levels of competency in any of these areas relies upon the cumulative effect of many, many learning experiences provided in and out of the classroom and across the institution. Success requires amounts of practice and feedback that are orders of magnitude higher than most colleges and universities now demand or provide. Note that a commitment to address these core learning outcomes across the curriculum and at all levels is in and of itself a shift in faculty and institutional culture; the commitment requires that faculty members accept responsibility and accountability for demanding practice in and mastery of those desired competencies in all courses and for providing timely and appropriate feedback *on those competencies* to students in their courses. That means, for example, that professors who require writing projects in classes in the major provide feedback to students about their writing, as well as about their grasp of the specific disciplinary content. It also means that residence life professional staff must hold resident assistants to standards of quality in their written reports. The point is that in an institution with a culture of serious teaching and learning, educators of all kinds and in all contexts share responsibility for ensuring that students are challenged to achieve excellence.

Problem-Based Learning

Students often have more motivation to learn when they can understand the application of new knowledge to real world problems. Problem-based learning, a powerful pedagogy commonly used in graduate and professional education in medicine and other health sciences, law, business, engineering, and architecture addresses this opportunity by clearly demonstrating the links between theory and practice. Problem-based learning has complex theoretical roots and a lineage that includes the work of Alfred North Whitehead (who rejected the notion that the mind stores inert ideas and wrote, "Education is the acquisition of the art of the utilization of knowledge"[24]) and John Dewey, who closely linked experience and education in educational theory and practice. Problem-based learning asks students to use and apply what they learn in real time; it forces both faculty and students to integrate ideas, think critically and creatively, carefully define a problem, and construct an appropriate and relevant solution. It also creates an opportunity for research-oriented faculty members to engage students in solving the real problems they are working on—thus enabling students to benefit directly from learning in a scholarly, research-intensive institution. A specific application of problem-based learning on many campuses is the development of general education science courses as inquiries into specific pressing public problems, such as global warming, environmental protection and sustainability, and epidemics of disease; by exploring the dimensions of—and often collecting data about—a large public problem, students are introduced to the scientific principles, methods, and data that may provide solutions to that problem.

Comprehensive Examinations

Most universities require doctoral students to pass comprehensive examinations to demonstrate mastery of a prescribed body of knowledge in an integrated and synthetic way. We recommend a similar requirement for students at two points in their undergraduate programs:

- Near the end of the second (sophomore) year, students should demonstrate their mastery of the works on a core curriculum reading list by writing an essay (note: not objective, multiple choice) examination. The faculty will have created the reading list in the process of developing the required core curriculum; students will have encountered and used the works on the list throughout their general education experience, in multiple courses; specific works may or may not have been recommended or required in specific courses, but the list would signal to students what the faculty feels are exemplary pieces with which all students should be familiar as they prepare to enter the great conversation. In the comprehensive examination, given in the closing weeks of the fourth semester (or sixth quarter) in a take-home format, students would be required to demonstrate not only content mastery, but also good writing, critical thinking, analysis of sources and problems, and the integration and synthesis of knowledge across disciplines. The combination of the core curriculum, reading list, and comprehensive examination would abolish any misconception about the lack of importance of general education while affirming the faculty's priority on students achieving mastery in broad learning domains.

- As part of the capstone (or, as we prefer to say, keystone—see next section) experience in the final year, students should demonstrate mastery in each major. The faculty in each discipline—or, in the case of interdisciplinary majors, in two of more disciplines—would determine the texts or other materials and resources to be mastered by all students in their majors. A comprehensive examination in written, oral, or a combined format would demonstrate students' achievement of mastery.

Keystone (Capstone) Experience

It is a current trend in higher education to require a capstone learning experience for undergraduates in their final year, usually in the form of senior seminars and/or a required thesis or project. As might be expected, the intensity and quality of these capstone experiences varies a great deal both within and across institutions. We choose to elevate the expectations of such experiences and call them "keystone," rather than capstone, learning events. A keystone, in architecture, is the critical piece that is set at the top, or crown, or an arch to stabilize the entire structure and lock the other pieces into place. The keystone, unlike one of many capstones, is what really holds everything together; when shaped and placed properly, it creates a stable final product that is always in tension but also in equilibrium. By analogy, a keystone learning product, to bring stability to an educational program, or structure, must demonstrate mastery in a field of study while also providing final evidence of knowledge and competency in writing, critical thinking, and other cognitive skills, and the assumptions and culture of the discipline. A keystone learning experience, when done well, evokes pride in the student, faculty, and institution. As noted previously, we recommend a comprehensive oral or written examination at the conclusion of the keystone course.

Learning Portfolios

Learning portfolios are important tools that support and document student learning.[25] In either print or electronic format (there are both homegrown and proprietary electronic, and usually web-based, products for these), learning portfolios provide a structured, intentional way for students to archive the products and artifacts of their learning, reflect on the learning that has occurred, develop and demonstrate self-assessment skills, and select pieces of work that best illustrate and exemplify their mastery of learning goals. A learning portfolio should contain evidence of learning in both courses and outside-the-classroom learning experiences, and the same expectations of reflection, assessment, and selection of the best work apply to each. Portfolios have allowed colleges and universities to effectively document—and, in some cases, give credit for—learning that occurs in leadership development programs, residence halls, student employment, service learning, and so on. The learning portfolio, if done well, offers a particularly rich and flexible method of documenting learning far beyond test scores, course grades, and cumulative grade point averages; it also reinforces students' responsibility and accountability for their own learning, which furthers their development as self-directed learners and advances their progress on the pathway from novice to expert, and it creates a structure for collaboration with and mentoring by faculty and professional staff. A primary requirement for the effective use of learning portfolios is for faculty, student affairs professionals, advisors, and others who have been engaged with a student to conduct periodic reviews of the material archived in the portfolio and to discuss the growing portfolio with their colleagues—and with the student—as a way of assessing completion of goals as well as continuing the design of a program of study that will address new or expanded goals.

Conclusion

We offer the concepts, guiding principles, educational models, and curricular and pedagogical practices described in this chapter to catalyze discussion. If adopted as a package and applied rigorously, we believe they would provide a far more significant undergraduate education than now exists in most American higher education. Far more students would experience truly transformative higher learning.

There is little that is new or radical in the individual elements of what we have proposed; what *is* radical is that we propose it as a whole, to be developed and instituted (in the most literal sense of that word) at scale for all undergraduates. Taken together, the elements we have suggested would support cumulative learning according to a common view among faculty about what constitutes an exemplary, distinctive, and distinguished undergraduate education. Students, faculty, and staff would experience higher education differently; they would encounter high expectations for the quality and quantity of work (publicly articulated and communicated before admission), rigorous standards, and a campuswide preoccupation with learning itself—all features of a renewed educational culture. The institution would have intentionally created that culture—a culture of serious teaching and learning—and immersed students in it; adapting to their immersion, students would become apprentices in higher learning, gradually gaining authority and autonomy as learners under the tutelage and mentorship of caring, but demanding, faculty members.

Instituted as intended—as guiding principles for an entire undergraduate program—the model and practices we suggest would improve retention, enhance admissions, and demonstrably improve student learning. Needless to say, what we have recommended has significant implications for institutional priorities, the use of resources, incentive and reward systems for faculty and students, and the organization, structure, and operations of colleges and universities. We appreciate that what we are espousing requires substantial—even dramatic—institutional change. We turn to that subject in the next chapter.

7

Talk of Change Is Not Change

Rethinking American Higher Education

A Call for Rethinking Higher Education

What is wrong with undergraduate higher education in the United States cannot be "fixed" in any of the usual senses of that word. Most recent proposals for reforming higher education miss the real point by focusing on reducing costs and increasing productivity and efficiency in one way or another. Each approach has its own fierce advocates and cynical detractors, but all of them circle the real target—the insufficient quality and quantity of learning in higher education—at some distance. The most commonly recommended strategy—infusing tough-minded business principles to improve management accountability—would produce nicer financial statements while continuing to divert attention from what is really needed: a complete rethinking of higher education.

As we explained in the previous chapter, the problem is one of value, not costs. But it is far easier to think of various schemes to reduce costs than to engage the tough questions about purpose, expectations, and outcomes in higher education. So we have proposals to shorten the baccalaureate curriculum to three years, offer low-cost bachelor's degrees by eliminating various alleged frills (such as opportunities for personal contact with faculty members or advisors), replace traditional classroom instruction with online courses or programs, and increase the productivity of professors. Not surprisingly, faculty tenure, alleged administrative bloat, and student services are frequent and easy targets for cost cutters. But all fiscally based proposals are really distractions, not true reforms; even if the nuggets of reasonability hidden in each of them were lifted up and implemented effectively, we would have only institutions that more efficiently fail to produce higher learning.

Proposed strategies that emphasize cost cutting might be especially dangerous if they actually worked—that is, if they succeeded in increasing operational efficiency. The accommodations made in the interest of lower costs would probably worsen the already critical condition of higher learning in higher education. Given the upside-down priorities in place on many campuses, the sacrifices demanded to cut costs might well come from academic programs, full-time faculty, and services that support student learning—not from offices that worry about rankings, competition with other institutions, consumer satisfaction, marketing, and image management. Few institutions would cancel plans to build a new stadium in order to ensure the construction of additional classrooms.

Consensus has begun to form among most thoughtful critics, inside or outside the academy on this point: it is no longer possible to think of making any real difference in higher education through minor adjustments or tweaks. There is an increasingly common recognition that truly fundamental change is needed—that something must be done and that the something has to be larger, more systematic and systemic, and far more universal than one little change here and another little change there. We are beyond fixes, cheap or otherwise. A simple, formulaic cost-cutting plan just won't work.

In choosing the title of this book, the authors wanted to emphasize the need for such a systematic and systemic approach. We were not simply being inflammatory without purpose. Neither our assessment of the gravity and urgency of the problem—"we're losing our minds"— nor our proposed solution—"rethinking higher education"—suggests a predominantly economic analysis or a primarily fiscal solution. Increasing efficiency will not stop the unacceptable loss of potential and opportunity for our students, and it will not accomplish what is so desperately needed—a thorough and candid rethinking of higher education itself. We intended to make it clear that what our nation is facing in higher education today is an actual emergency and that effectively confronting and responding to that emergency demands far more than fine tuning. "We're losing our minds" is an extraordinary judgment to make, and "rethinking higher education" rightly suggests that there is no easy or superficial solution. The title and this book are intended to be a call to action.

Higher Education Must Change

We need to rethink higher education. There is nothing easy or incremental about what must be done. Rethinking higher education means questioning the entire pantheon of assumptions, principles, priorities, values, organizational structures, reward systems, and usual and customary practices that are the common foundation for undergraduate programs. It means starting from the position that nothing that currently is assumed or in place about undergraduate education, from faculty roles and responsibilities to general education curricula and community service programs, is exempt from a comprehensive reexamination and revision in the interest of learning.

What we propose is decidedly *not* incremental. It is not small scale. It will not be easy, fast, or painless. Everything colleges and universities do that is *not* teaching and learning deserves new scrutiny. In fact, the only thing that deserves even closer scrutiny is everything that colleges and universities now do that *is*—or at least is claimed or understood to be—teaching and learning. That is what rethinking higher education means. But there's more.

Rethinking higher education also means rigorously identifying, evaluating, and challenging the many damaging accommodations that colleges and universities, individually and collectively, have made (and continue to make) to consumer and competitive pressures, especially during the last two or three decades. We mean the allocation of increasing proportions of institutional resources to facilities and grounds, personnel, programs, and activities that do not directly and significantly contribute to the kind of holistic, developmental, and transformative learning that we defined as higher learning in earlier chapters. We mean the enormous expenditures devoted purely to securing a better ranking in the magazine surveys. We mean the progressive reduction in academic, intellectual, and behavioral expectations that has undermined the culture, learning conditions, and civility of so many campus communities. We mean the kind of thinking that elevates branding and marketing in importance and priority above educational programs and academic quality as ways to attract students and secure robust enrollments. We mean the deplorable practice of building attractive new buildings while offering lackluster first- and second-year courses taught primarily by poorly paid and dispirited contingent faculty. We mean the assumption that retention is just keeping students in school longer, without serious regard for the quality of their learning or their cumulative learning outcomes at graduation. We mean giving priority to intercollegiate sports programs while support for the success of the great majority of students who are not intercollegiate athletes suffers.

These accommodations are expensive and in more than one way; they cost a lot of money, cause distraction from the true mission of higher education, divert attention from needed educational reforms, reinforce unwarranted and unrealistic consumer expectations, and replace sound educational standards with oversimplified and often unfounded operational metrics. It is these accommodations that have given root to and now sustain the truly dangerous idea that degrees are simply deliverables, bought with tuition.

Saying that higher education has to change is easy. We are by no means the first to do it, and, if ideas such as ours are not noticed and taken seriously, do not achieve traction, and fail to inspire a broad public conversation, we will not be the last. Saying that change is needed is actually not even controversial today, given the torrent of critiques the academy has recently encountered and endured. Talk about change is easy, frequent, and increasingly predictable—but talk is not enough; talk is not change. Defining the specifications of the needed changes, and describing the ways in which they could be practically and effectively achieved, and— especially—executing them at scale across the diversity of institutional types are much more challenging tasks.

Systemic Cultural Change in Higher Education

The current culture—the human construction of shared norms, values, standards, expectations, priorities—of teaching and learning in the academy is not powerful enough to support true higher learning.

Without a strong, serious culture of teaching and learning, students do not experience the kind of integrated, holistic, developmental, rigorous undergraduate education that must exist as an absolute condition for truly transformative higher learning to occur. We do not demand enough (doing that would conflict with consumer friendliness, perhaps), our standards are not high enough (having them higher would undermine retention for a few years, probably), we accept half-hearted work from students who do not insist on enough from themselves and do not know how to ask for more from their teachers (doing otherwise would make college more serious; how could it still be fun?). Degrees have become deliverables because we are no longer willing to make students work hard against high standards to earn them.

A weak educational culture creates all the wrong opportunities. Without academic expectations to bring structure to students' time, too much time is wasted. In the absence of high academic and behavioral expectations, less demanding peer norms become dominant. In the peer culture, time spent on classwork, reading, and reflection must be limited; too much of it becomes a stain on a student's social value. It has become possible—even likely—to survive academically, be retained in school, get passing grades, and graduate with a baccalaureate despite long-term patterns of alcohol and other substance abuse that are known to damage the formation of new memories and reduce both students' capacity and readiness to learn. The atmosphere of too many residence halls drives serious students out of their own rooms (functionally, their on-campus homes) to study, write, reflect, and think. It is as yet hard to discern exactly how new and emerging digital environments—notably, social networking technologies that privilege either anonymity or extraordinary openness without clear boundaries—will challenge traditional assumptions about moral, ethical, and identity development.

What *is* clear is that unacceptably low expectations make unstructured time abundant, and that today's full-time, traditional-age undergraduate students have more than enough of both distractions and unstructured time. The other commitments (work, commuting, family responsibilities, participation in other community or volunteer service, etc.) of returning adults and other part-time undergraduates greatly reduce the amount of unstructured time in their lives and also distract them from their academic engagements. They may require more time to complete their academic programs, but expectations of them should nonetheless be high and standards for their performance must still be rigorous. In other words, the presence of time-consuming distractions, no matter how legitimate, does not justify reducing expectations of students or the rigor of programs.

As a society we allow—in fact, condone—institutional policies, practices, and systems in higher education that, taken together, make good teaching a heroic act performed by truly dedicated faculty members rather than the universal expectation and norm across campuses. Similarly, we allow the most regressive features of undergraduate culture to undermine the motivation and desire for intellectual growth of many good students; in many ways, being a serious student is also a heroic act. We allow passivity to dominate students' already slight engagement with courses and faculty. We acknowledge with despair the constraints that prevent most colleges and universities from hiring and retaining enough full-time faculty members to ensure the long-term quality of their undergraduate educational programs—but we fail to look closely enough at what they *did* spend money on. The money went somewhere—just not to teaching and learning.

The real issue is not that higher education has become a business, as is commonly charged within the academy, or that it has emerged from its recent struggles having too much corporate character. The issue is that the attention of higher education is no longer focused on its most important responsibility: learning. The current culture of colleges and universities no longer puts learning first—and in most institutions, that culture perpetuates a fear of doing so. Across the spectrum of American higher education, we do not have a serious culture of teaching and learning. Isolated examples to the contrary exist, but are only the exceptions that prove the rule. The leaders of many, if not most, colleges and universities might agree, but would also say, with some justice, that no single institution can risk being the only one to change; that restoring attention to the fundamentals, rather than the frills, would put that one institution at serious risk. It is true that this is a collective problem; action by many schools, supported by a strong national impetus for change, is needed.

In calling for the kind of serious, systemic rethinking that directly and unflinchingly accepts the challenge of improving undergraduate higher education, we are asking for three things; taken together, they demand

and would produce a profound, needed, and overdue cultural change in our colleges and universities.

1. The widespread acceptance and application of a new and better touchstone for decision making in higher education, linked to a strong framework of essential, core principles, as suggested in the previous chapter. A touchstone is a standard, or criterion, that serves as the basis for judging something; in higher education, that touchstone must be *the quality and quantity of learning*. A touchstone and a clear conceptual framework are important because we need to link our advocacy for change to a powerful set of ideas, commitments, and principles against which to test current policies, practices, and proposals for reform.

2. A comprehensive reevaluation of undergraduate education and experience guided by those core principles. This must occur both nationally, as an essential public conversation, and within the walls of institutions of all types and sizes; it must be supported by boards of trustees, higher education professional organizations, and regional accrediting bodies alike.

3. The actual implementation of needed reforms and renewal of undergraduate higher education, informed by the reevaluation and public conversation and enacted through decisions based on the new touchstone, improving the quality and quantity of learning.

Both the process and the results of a serious rethinking of higher education will be more likely to succeed and less likely to cause unwanted harm if that rethinking is generated by an authentic public discussion linked to and supporting cultural change in colleges and universities than if it is imposed by a disappointed, frustrated nation through its legislative and regulatory authority. Levels of dissatisfaction with the priorities and outcomes of higher education among parents, alumni, employers, and elected officials are unlikely to decline absent significant reform; better efficiency and lower costs, even if achieved, will produce only short-term relief. Cultural change from within, across the entire spectrum and expanse of higher education, will be disruptive, but has the unique promise of restoring higher learning in higher education while preserving its extraordinary diversity. Without such change, external interventions and demands that will be far more disruptive and far less tolerant of institutional diversity become increasingly likely.

Learning: The Essential Touchstone for Decision Making

In the previous chapter, we outlined a framework of ten principles for a culture of higher learning and eight components of a distinguished program of liberal education within such a culture. We argued that instituted in an integrated manner, as intended—and therefore serving as guiding principles for an entire undergraduate program—these policies and practices would enhance admissions, improve retention, and demonstrably strengthen student learning and success. Central to both the ten principles and the eight program components is a commitment to making learning the highest priority in higher education.

Learning is, sadly, not currently the touchstone for decision making in higher education. Every day members of governing boards, presidents and chancellors, vice presidents, provosts, deans, department chairs, and student affairs professionals have to analyze options and make decisions. Which do you want: More full-time faculty members and new academic programs or an addition to the recreation center? More study abroad opportunities, expanded student aid, or more performers with greater name recognition booked in campus venues? More professional development options for faculty and staff or more advanced technologies in classrooms and teaching laboratories? More attractive landscaping and more frequent maintenance of grounds or expansion of the collections of the libraries? Fewer adjunct and part-time faculty members or more academic advisors? More professional counselors or less waiting time at computer labs? More students, better prepared students, or both? Guns, butter, or some of each? How much should the president, the athletic director, a new assistant professor, or a contingent faculty member be paid? How many positions at one level do we have to leave unfilled in order to fill one position at another level?

Adding stress to difficult choices such as these is the raw fact that today, many institutions—both public and private, large and small—have very limited financial flexibility as a consequence of a prolonged, painful recession and the havoc it continues to wreak: damaged endowments, reduced investment income, restricted direct or indirect government support, severe competition for enrollment, and limited tuition and fee increases. For some, other factors also apply—overly optimistic projections about national and global economic futures, loan or bonding deals that were attractive only a few years ago but now seem ridiculously expensive in a new economic context, and the planning and development of expensive overseas campuses. For other institutions, excessively enthusiastic enrollment predictions made in the past have introduced greater complexity in the form of now-regretted and painfully costly expansions of facilities, programs, enrollments, or staff. More than one university has entertained the possibility of selling some of its key assets to balance the operating budget—and a few have done so. Having little financial wiggle room makes hard choices even more difficult; when an institution must choose to do only one or two things out of a long list of possibilities, the stakes are higher. Tough economic conditions, by increasing the stakes, also underscore the importance of clearly articulating the basis on which hard and necessary decisions will be made.

But today, choices about the allocation of resources in institutions of higher education are most often not about options for new programs, buildings, or staff at all. Many decisions now being considered and taken have a particularly negative character: which programs or positions to cut in order to accommodate dire financial conditions. To balance the budget, do we eliminate academic programs or lay off administrative or professional staff? Do we defer raises in faculty salaries or put off needed maintenance on campus buildings? Freeze hiring for regular tenure-track faculty, administrative staff, contingent faculty, or all of those groups? Make reductions in student support services or increases in the size of sections of core courses? Delays in new construction projects or reductions in the size and scope of a branch campus?

In every case and in all economic conditions, decisions about resources are forced choices, and every decision that has strategic implications is almost entirely about resources. The progress of colleges and universities toward new or different goals, like their ways of surviving in tough times, is always powered by resources of one kind or another. In the end, all of those decisions must reflect leaders' understanding and expression of institutional priorities and values; in that way, they are moral choices, and budgets are moral documents. The fundamental question underlying every such choice is just this: What is most important to us? Consider the following examples.

- If rising in the magazine rankings has highest priority, a review of items included in the scales used by the magazines to do their rankings can be used to constitute a kind of needs assessment. Institutional leaders will determine that they need to add this, or expand that, or preserve something else, or correct some other thing, so the school will rank higher next year than it did this year—or, at least, not slip lower. Since the magazines' criteria do not include anything that directly measures the quality or quantity of learning, any impact of decisions to allocate resources toward improving rankings will have at best only indirect and secondary benefits for learning. Of course having more in one place usually means having less somewhere else, as well, so, in many cases, assigning priority to rankings will drive decisions that negatively affect learning. And never mind the probability that competing institutions are conducting the same analysis and trying to elevate or sustain their own status in the rankings, too. As schools all work toward more of something in order to improve their rankings, the implied baseline rises as well, because there is no *standard* for good or better or best. Rankings are based on comparisons, after all, so, over time, having more in some area has less and less meaning in real terms—it only means more than other similar colleges have, regardless of the impact or importance of more.
- If expanding enrollment is the main priority, which is often the case in tuition-dependent public and private institutions, it may take more than reviewing the criteria used in magazine rankings to sufficiently identify what needs to be done. Predictions of demographic trends, market surveys, student satisfaction data, and price analyses may add other parameters that must be given attention in order to create messages and activities that will draw more students to the institution. Responding to enrollment challenges and demands often results in the acquisition of an entire corps of staff members whose job it is to bring more students in: branding, marketing, communications, prospecting, recruiting, and so on. Which, of course, means that there is less money available to hire other people into other positions, such as full-time faculty. One unfortunate consequence of enrollment-driven decision making may be that more students matriculate but are taught primarily by poorly paid contingent faculty members (and/or research-oriented faculty members who are unable or unwilling to

take student learning seriously); another may be a decline in the quality or preparedness of admitted students.

- If becoming a top 50 or top 100 institution in some category—such as research-intensive universities—has highest priority, very different decisions will be made than if increasing undergraduate enrollment, getting better rankings, or improving the undergraduate experience is the primary goal. Attention must be paid (and therefore resources must be allocated) to recruiting high-quality research faculty members, protecting the time of those faculty members (a euphemism for making sure they do not have to teach or spend much time with undergraduates, especially in introductory courses or general education), creating a robust research infrastructure, offering stipends and assistantships to graduate students, and competing successfully for federal research awards (and dollars). Once again, the obvious questions are often ignored: Is there one of the existing top 50 or top 100 schools in the same category that no longer wishes to maintain that status? If not, which of the current members of those exclusive clubs is weak enough to be knocked out by an upstart arrival? And, by the way, what other institutions that are not currently in the top 50 or top 100 might also be gunning for a chance to get there? Not to mention this conundrum: What happens to the supply of excellent graduate students if the undergraduate programs are weakened by an emphasis on research? In most cases, universities that aspire to high status as research institutions must divert resources (money, faculty, space, and emphasis) from undergraduate programs in order to achieve their goals. It is easy to say that it should be possible to do both, and the best research universities often have exceptional undergraduate programs—but building a strong research program where one did not previously exist will almost always be done at the expense of the undergraduate programs.

The point is just this: that all decisions in higher education, as elsewhere in our society, are made against some touchstone—some generally understood and agreed upon set of priorities that enables leaders to choose more of this and less of that. Touchstones embody operational purposes, whether or not those purposes are reflected in the actual institutional mission and vision statements; no serious college or university would say their mission was to rise in the magazine rankings or enroll more students. But whether or not they are written down in any such official or sanctioned way, the priorities that comprise a touchstone for decision making identify what it is that people in leadership roles think the college or university is supposed to accomplish, and those priorities may therefore have far more operational significance than the mission statement itself. So it is that mission and purposes, on the one hand, have so often become disconnected from operational priorities, on the other. In those circumstances, the mission statement becomes simply a brand marker, evidence of what the institution thinks it should be doing, or what it should say it is doing, regardless of what it actually does and values. And in the end the priority assigned to teaching and learning in the mission statement is seldom matched by patterns of resource allocation for undergraduate education.

Strategic decisions may be more or less difficult, depending on institutional conditions; having less to work with may make decisions strangely easier or much harder. But in all three of the examples noted previously, it is at least possible to determine whether the decisions made have produced the outcome desired. In the first instance—elevating the college's standing in the magazine rankings—the measure of success is easy to identify and simple to ascertain, if not to achieve: a change (theoretically, a positive change) in the rankings. In the second, the key metric is also accessible and definitive: levels of enrollment in some category of students over the next one or two or future years. While the time frame for the third is much longer—getting to the top 50 or top 100 is unlikely in any short term, unless an institution is now no. 51 or no. 101—the ultimate measure of success is also easy to identify and track. In many ways the ease of measurement makes the touchstone work, and not only in an assessment sense; colleges and universities can rally staff, and sometimes faculty, around tangible, measurable institutional goals such as enrollment or comparative status. One might argue, in fact, that the ease of measurement privileges these goals among other potential institutional priorities ("what gets measured gets done"); other goals that might also matter—and sometimes matter a great deal—may not have such convincing and convenient metrics, and so do not get addressed. This is another reason that operations can so easily lose sight of mission and purpose; while the mission statement creates priorities that are sometimes frustratingly vague, operational priorities that are easily measurable have an acuity and credibility that is granted by the very fact of their being exactly that, operational. What you see is what you get, and what you cannot easily see you might as well not get.

For real change to occur, the quality and quantity of learning must replace any of those others as the key touchstone for decision making in higher education. It is both as simple and as difficult as that. We have made the case that the problem we face in higher education is the quality and quantity of learning. It is in ensuring that resources are allocated to improving learning that the solutions will be found, and it is in the careful, rigorous assessment of learning that proof of the effectiveness and value of those solutions can be sought. So every major or strategic decision—any choice that affects how resources are allocated and used—must be made not only in the context of learning, but with explicit, direct exploration and explication of the consequences of that decision for the quality and quantity of learning and of the ways in which those consequences can be assessed and documented.

Comprehensive Review of Undergraduate Higher Education

Consider what is required for such substantial and fundamental change to occur—for there to be a broad reconsideration and renewal of values, priorities, and operating principles throughout higher education; for leaders in colleges and universities to put learning ahead of other considerations and to sustain that priority; and for patterns of resource allocation on our campuses to alter course dramatically. Replacing one touchstone with another is itself a radical cultural shift; for that shift to happen, the public, elected and appointed officials, professional organizations in higher education, the regional accrediting bodies, and, most importantly, administrators, professional staff, and faculty members in colleges and universities must not only recognize the existing deficiencies in higher learning within higher education, but also demand—or, at least, support, or provide support for—significant institutional change to address those deficiencies.

Culture is a human construct. It is always built of shared values and implicit or explicit agreements among people who share some basis for interactions—historic, demographic, geographic, social, spiritual, economic, political, or, now, digital. Sometimes, but not always, those shared values or agreements are documented, as in the U.S. Constitution, the Declaration of Independence, the Bible, the bylaws of organizations, or the rules of engagement for the allowable use of certain social media. Usually, though, culture is created from less formal but deeply meaningful connections among people who feel the relational force of certain important bonds.

So it is that culture change almost always starts with the most basic of human interactions—in conversations, which may be discussions between two or among several or a lot of people, in any format and through any medium, about an event, idea, or issue of shared concern. The conversations may be scholarly, rancorous, civil, calm, pointed, antagonistic, constructive, or angry; the only requirement—not that such a requirement can actually be imposed—is that they be intentional (i.e., that they purposefully address concerns about a particular issue, such as the need for change in higher education). These conversations must occur repeatedly, involving as many people as possible from the whole spectrum of constituents concerned about an issue and connected as a culture. Over time, the outcomes from many of these discussions build a matrix, or web, of shared knowledge, experience, and analysis that may provide an impetus for actual change.

This process of change must occur in and around institutions of higher education of all kinds, sizes, and purposes, wherever they are, however they are governed, and by whatever means they are funded. That is why a vibrant, honest, and powerful public conversation about our goals and expectations for higher education is essential. Systemic, nationwide change in higher education requires more than individual, local campus discussions; expectations must change everywhere, on campuses all across the nation, not just in a few regions, state systems, or institutions.

The progress of a change of this magnitude can be envisioned as a wave moving across the landscape of higher education; at any given moment, institutions may be at very different points on the wave. The wave of change will of course not reach every school at the same time or even in the same year. It is probable that the impact of the wave will be felt differently on some campuses than others and that some colleges will feel the force of the wave earlier, or more powerfully, than others. But what matters for cultural change is that we, collectively, cause that wave—that we have a large-scale national conversation that focuses our attention on higher education in a serious way and that we have that conversation and maintain our focus for long enough to start other waves of change within state systems, in regions, among groups of peer institutions, and on individual campuses.

Questions like the ones that follow will inform and drive the conversations that instigate these waves of change:

- What are our common, collective expectations for undergraduate higher education? That is, what knowledge, personal qualities, abilities, attitudes, commitments, and values do we expect college graduates to have—no matter where they went to school? What do we think we (students, parents, employers, society) should rightfully be able to expect of any college graduate?

- Are those expectations being met today? Do college graduates come to employers, government service, or graduate and professional schools prepared to succeed? To what extent are we satisfied with what students have learned while engaged in higher education? Can new graduates think critically? Do they communicate well orally and in writing? Can they work in teams?

- What evidence do we have about what students have learned in college? Can we compare what, and how well, students learn in different institutions? Do we have evidence that students learn more, or better, or differently in one kind of institution versus others? In small liberal arts colleges versus comprehensive universities? Can we define any parameters that clearly distinguish institutions from each other on the grounds of the value they provide, if value is defined by the quality and quantity of learning?

- Are the priorities of our colleges and universities aligned with our expectations about the quality and quantity of learning that students should experience and achieve while enrolled? Are we comfortable with recent, current, and projected patterns of resource allocation in higher education? Do leaders in the academy invest in the right things to support learning? Do they make the same decisions that we would, if we wanted to advance learning?

- How can we, as a nation, ensure that our significant, ongoing investments in higher education are producing good returns? Given the size and scope of federal and state expenditures in higher education is there sufficient accountability?

- Can we restore a strong emphasis on learning in higher education without somehow undermining the academy's two other major roles—research and service? Should research-intensive universities be exempt from our general expectations about learning among undergraduates? If not, how do we ensure that undergraduate education gets sufficient attention in those schools? Is it really necessary to have significant research programs in so many institutions? Are there better ways to support productive scholars and researchers than the ones we use now?

- How competitive are the graduates of our undergraduate programs when compared to graduates of similar programs in other countries? Are we maintaining our leadership in science, technology, engineering, and mathematics (STEM) fields? Do our graduates have sufficient preparation in the liberal arts to make them well-rounded people who can get things done in the world?

- Does the overall undergraduate experience effectively address the needs of students for learning outside the classroom and for their development as whole people? Do college graduates generally have a good sense of their own identity? Are they able to maintain sound relationships? Do they provide evidence of solid moral and ethical development? Are they prepared to be good, contributing citizens? Can they take the perspective of others? Are they prepared to live and work in an increasingly global, worldwide culture?

- Can we ensure some level of consistency in undergraduate higher education, and in the qualities and abilities of college graduates, without undermining the essential diversity of colleges and universities and without eroding the ability of individual institutions to establish and maintain their own distinctiveness?

For real change to occur, discussions about the quality and quantity of learning in higher education and the need for reform must occur at multiple levels, in many places, and over a significant period of time. A broad public conversation may be generated by attention in the broadcast and cable media (talk and interview shows, special reports, case studies of individual institutions by local and regional reporters), in the traditional press (opinion pieces and reports on the work and outcomes of colleges and universities in the coverage area of the newspaper or other publication), and through comments and interactions on websites, blogs, and email. The public conversation (by which we mean the whole mass of such conversations, occurring asynchronously but generally contemporaneously) may inspire—or be inspired and reinforced by—discussions in government (think of debates about proposals for changes in federal, state, or city statutes or regulations and hearings in statehouses or Congress), higher education organizations of any kind, and the regional accrediting associations.

Still, the most important arena in which these conversations ultimately have to occur is on campuses themselves. The country has the right to expect higher education to lead such a discussion. Administrators, academic leaders, faculty members, professional staff, and students, in various groups and combinations, should participate actively and contribute meaningfully to discussions about the quality and quantity of learning on *their* campus. The national conversation provides context, direction, and motive—but only many intimate and passionate conversations among colleagues can ground the discussion enough to give it the power to bring change. Any number of events or circumstances can start these conversations, including the following:

- a strategic planning process that fully engages all sectors of the institution
- a significant change in institutional leadership—usually the transition of the president or the provost
- the review of key institutional data, such as findings from student surveys concerning learning, engagement, or satisfaction
- changes in the institution's performance on enrollment or important parameters of persistence and retention
- self-study for first or renewed accreditation and/or a candid report from an accreditation team
- responses to financial challenges or crises requiring reassessment of programs and the reallocation of resources
- changes in the character or priorities of the governing board
- results of assessments of student learning

- strong interest of individual faculty members in improving teaching and learning
- pressure from students, parents, alumni, employers, trustees, or others
- one or more professional or faculty development presentations about learning, the assessment of learning, and the quality and quantity of learning in higher education
- proposed or planned changes in the mix of faculty—especially reductions in the number or proportion of tenure-track faculty and increases in the number or proportion of non-tenure-track and contingent faculty
- revision of the faculty handbook or of policies regarding faculty hiring, reappointment, promotion, and tenure
- proposed or planned changes in faculty workload
- proposed or planned additions to faculty responsibilities for advising—or the hiring of professional, rather than faculty, advisors
- discussions among faculty members about changes in the level of civility in classrooms

There is an almost predictable pattern to the sequence of these essential conversations once they begin on most campuses. Resistance to the idea that there is anything wrong, and therefore strong doubt about the need to change anything, is especially common in early discussions among and with members of the faculty, even—or perhaps particularly—when a faculty champion or consultant initiates them. The presentation of evidence to support claims that a problem exists may, but does not necessarily, weaken that resistance. Some observers will claim that any evidence presented is flawed by poorly collected, analyzed, or applied data, or, if comparative data are used, that the situation in their institution is so unique that no data from elsewhere could possibly be applicable or informative. Cynical claims about the motives of the colleagues who instigated the discussion or collected and reported the data follow quickly; some irascible administrators, staff, or faculty usually make veiled threats of one kind or another, or may simply leave the conversation. But as the many conversations continue and deepen, other faculty members, staff, or administrators begin to voice more progressive positions in favor of change, and, over time, more of their colleagues begin to move toward and then may adopt those positions as well.

It is unlikely that this process of cultural change on any campus can succeed without strong leadership from respected faculty members, academic department chairs and deans, and the senior academic officer. A sound process also requires commitment and full participation by the senior student affairs officer. The president should be supportive, and indeed may help initiate, but usually will not lead such a process. Patience on the part of those who instigated the process is essential; enough time must be given to allow the gradual steps of widening and deepening the conversation about reform and renewal to occur. Advancing too quickly simply inspires greater resistance, can convert allies to enemies, and may reduce the chance of a good outcome. Moving too slowly sacrifices the advantages of momentum.

The commitment, enthusiasm, and passion of newly appointed full-time faculty members often fuels both the instigation of cultural change and progress toward its goals. These new instructors or assistant professors on the tenure track frequently feel a particular connection to undergraduates and make special accommodations to advise and mentor them. Since they often have come from other institutions, they may have a fresh perspective; not yet burdened by the weight of local history, they may be more optimistic about both the potential of students and the possibility for institutional change than are their more seasoned colleagues. The challenge they face, of course, is built into systems of faculty evaluation, reappointment, promotion, and tenure; in most colleges and universities, advising, mentoring, spending extra time with students, and focusing on the success of undergraduates are not among the criteria for advancement. The time of a faculty member is finite, and priorities must be set; time spent advising and coaching undergraduates is not devoted to research and scholarship—excellence in which definitely is among the criteria for advancement. It is, therefore, all too possible for the enthusiasm and commitment of these newer faculty members to be dangerous to their own success—and they will often get counsel from department chairs and more senior faculty to that effect.

Continued high levels of engagement with undergraduates by tenure-track faculty members may be, depending on one's perspective, heroic or self-destructive. Once institutional change has occurred, such engagement may no longer require heroism and may not be self-destructive. But all colleges and universities need to address the realities faced by untenured faculty members during the period of culture change in ways that preserve both their voices in the change process and their prospects for promotion and tenure.

From a systems point of view, the problem faced by change-oriented but untenured faculty has another, larger dimension. Newer, untenured faculty members have relatively little clout in the politics of faculties and universities. While they may be overcommitted with committee and working group assignments that their more senior peers have learned to avoid (or acquired the stature to refuse), they are seldom engaged with discussions at policy level and are rarely elected to representative bodies, such as faculty senates, through which they might gain power. Their advocacy for change therefore tends to stay localized, expressed within a particular professional development activity or department meeting; newer faculty members in different departments may hardly know each other, and there are few ways in which cross-departmental interaction might help them find out what their colleagues and peers in other departments are thinking and doing.

Even senior and tenured faculty members have to consider an important professional calculus in deciding whether to support—or, even more, instigate—discussions that might lead to substantial change in the fundamental culture of their institutions. For them, as for their more junior colleagues, there are only so many hours in the day; despite crabby allegations to the contrary by some commentators, tenured faculty members are usually fully occupied with their research and scholarship, university and public service, and teaching. Nurturing discussions about change requires its own change—in priorities and time allotments.

What, then, is the rationale for serious engagement by faculty members, junior or senior, tenured or untenured, in these discussions of undergraduate education? How does a professor justify devoting time, attention, and mindshare to processes that currently will not bring him or her any professional advantage? The answer is both obvious and difficult. Undergraduate higher education is not delivering true higher learning; students suffer every day because expectations are too low, rigor is nearly absent, standards are wanting, advising is insufficient, and learning is not the priority of their institutions. Conscientious faculty members—and most are exactly that—are concerned about students and their learning. Supporting student learning and success, which sounds ephemeral and vague in the abstract, is very real on the ground; most professors want the students they know to be successful. But most professors also work within an academic culture that does not support them in investing in student learning or caring about student success—even the success of the students they know personally. In those observations lie the motives for change—though in the same observations can be found the barriers. But the chance of developing a serious culture of teaching and learning is high enough, given enough discussion over enough time, that any faculty member who has thought through the tough issues raised in any discussion of undergraduate education should be able to see his or her place in both the process and the outcome.

Along this pathway of many discussions, faculty and others will necessarily and appropriately raise key questions about specific elements of institutional policy and practices. This is as it should and must be. Shifting institutional culture to focus on student learning inevitably raises pressing questions about faculty hiring, reappointment, promotion, and tenure that must be addressed and resolved, for example. Moving to a model of more interdisciplinary teaching and learning requires figuring out how to count the hours taught by each faculty member on the interdisciplinary team. Improving student advising and mentoring may create resource questions that have to be answered. In many universities, determining how to rebalance the historical blend of research, service, and teaching without devaluing any of the three will be the most critical and difficult step. It is especially important for institutions (and their advocates and critics) to avoid polarizing discussions of teaching and research, as if any university has to choose one to the exclusion of the other; far more nuanced conversations about the relative importance of research in colleges and universities of different types and missions are needed.

From the perspective of corporations (and, therefore, in the minds of many trustees), it will seem that the whole process of culture change is amazingly and unnecessarily protracted; the pace may seem indolent, and the many redundant discussions may appear precious and indulgent. But culture in higher education—like other cultures—does not change by force or the imposition of will. The very conservative nature and roots of the academy are the sources of some of its greatest strengths and are deeply connected to its mission.

Progress will not be made in improving the quality and quantity of learning—in restoring higher learning to higher education—unless both the public discussion and the multilayered, multistep processes of change on our campuses occur.

Reform and Renewal in Higher Education

The discussions held on each campus will take every institution on its own path toward reform and renewal to improve student learning. What is put in place in one institution will be true and resonant only for that institution; other schools will do something somewhat, or wildly, different. Institutional diversity is a strength of American higher education that should be celebrated and sustained. If the common purpose and theme of culture change is increasing the quality and quantity of learning, it is likely that most institutions will end up with certain similarities in their revised policies and practices, despite the fact that the specific renderings of those revisions might look different on every campus. The large-scale impact of these changes, in all their diversity, should be the creation of common, collective expectations and standards for higher learning that would apply across higher education.

When the touchstone is learning, decisions will be made differently than is true in most colleges and universities today. All of the forced choice questions that create strategic directions and determine the priorities in the day-to-day operations and management of higher education will demand a new kind of analysis and will have decidedly different outcomes. Institutions focused on learning will plan, operate, manage, and allocate resources differently than those that continue to emphasize magazine rankings, enrollment numbers, or their relative place in some categorization of institutions and purposes.

The colleges and universities that adopt learning as their highest priority will affirm that "learning comes first!" But what would an institution of higher education do differently if learning came first? How would it have changed? What will be the dimensions of a renewed institutional culture? How might students experience it differently?

In the ten principles of a serious culture of teaching and learning and the eight components of a renewed educational program recommended in the previous chapter are the answers—they are the goals and intended outcomes of renewal and reform. Here, we list elements of *evidence* that such reform is in progress—that substantial culture change has begun. We emphasize, however, that the list is not intended to serve as a linear schedule of what comes first, second, and next, nor is it exhaustive. The pace, outcomes, and evidence of culture change at each institution will vary depending on the presence and influence of all the factors that support or inhibit such change. As discussion of reform and renewal proceed, however, we might expect to see all or most of the following:

- Learning impact statements: Leaders would require the completion and submission of learning impact statements as part of every proposal for new or redirected resources. In these statements, administrators, faculty, or staff who ask for new positions, equipment, courses, academic or other programs, student services, or facilities—or for changes or reductions in any of those assets and resources—would specify the anticipated effects of the proposed actions on the quality and quantity of student learning and would provide evidence to support their proposal. By the time this process was firmly in place, it would be commonly understood throughout campus that proposals that, if implemented, would undermine or reduce the quality and quantity of learning in any serious way would not be approved or funded.

- Common student learning goals across all disciplines and departments: Faculty and professional staff from all the schools and colleges within the institution would have thought, met, talked, and reached strong consensus about the desired learning goals for the whole university—the cumulative learning outcomes expected of all students, regardless of major, such as critical thinking, problem solving, perspective taking, and effectiveness in oral and written communication—and would have communicated those goals to all students and to every educator who teaches, at any level. When asked, most faculty members and student affairs professionals would be able to speak about those learning goals, describe their importance, and define their own roles in helping students achieve them.

- Divisional, departmental, and program specific learning outcomes: The major divisions of the institution (notably academic affairs and student affairs) would have defined their own divisional learning outcomes, nested within and linked to the overall institutional outcomes, and departments in every division would have described their own intended learning outcomes, nested within and linked to the divisional outcomes, for minors, majors, programs, services, and activities. Departments (e.g., chemistry, English, geology, the counseling center, or career services) would have established highly specific learning outcomes for every program (such as a minor or major) and activity (such as leadership development). Students would know in advance through syllabi, descriptions of assignments, and information provided about experiential learning opportunities what they were expected to learn in every learning experience and how their achievement of those outcomes would be measured and reported. There would be no doubt about what the institution intended students to learn at any level.

- Revised and linked general education: The college's program of general education would have been revamped—or would be under review in anticipation of renewal. The archaic concept of general education as a separate, intellectually disconnected piece of an undergraduate's experience would have been replaced by the recognition that general education links with and continues through the majors and that the goals of general education are shared with those of the disciplines. Similarly, the use of distribution requirements as an organizing structure for general education would have been replaced by the development of core courses, which would be intentionally and strategically aligned with the institution's overall desired student learning outcomes. Students would no longer say that general education courses were "throwaway" classes that wasted their time.

- Elevated expectations and support for students: There would be much higher levels of both expectations and support for students. Students, responding to greatly improved and more comprehensive advising, would be making coherent, purposeful decisions about academic programs, courses, out-of-classroom learning experiences, internships, community service commitments, and, eventually, career options. Far less would be left to chance as students designed their learning plans.

- Rigorous and comprehensive assessment of student learning: A rigorous culture of assessment of learning would be in place throughout the institution. Professors and professional staff in student affairs would routinely assess the quality and quantity of student learning in learning experiences of every kind, inside and outside the classroom, in both formative and summative ways. Cumulative assessments of student learning in general education, minors and majors, and across the undergraduate experience, mapped against desired institutional student learning goals, would be completed regularly. Evidence of student learning for each student and for the aggregate of students in various categories would be collected and stored in electronic or paper portfolios.

- Student learning as basis for faculty and staff evaluation: Evidence of student learning would be routinely used in the evaluation of both faculty and staff; in the preparation of data to be shared with external parties, including the press and the media; and in the development of marketing, branding, and communications messages about the institution and its value to students and parents. If enough institutions were to begin collecting and using student learning assessment data, it would also become possible to compare colleges and universities based on learning effectiveness. If and when that were to occur, one or more of the magazines and newspapers that currently rate and rank institutions using other criteria might respond by piloting and then implementing rankings based on evidence of learning—at which point the public would have the first legitimate and meaningful comparisons of institutions.

- Purposeful closing of the assessment loop: Members of the faculty and staff would definitively close the loop in the assessment process, using the data obtained by measuring student learning to plan, complete, and deploy improvements in educational programs. Reassessments of learning after those improvements were made would be used to determine the effectiveness of actions taken; this cycle of assessment and improvement would be repeated as needed to assure teachers and leaders that every learning experience met critical tests of efficacy.

- Codified policies on faculty work: Institutional policy, as reflected in the faculty handbook and in each faculty member's employment contract, would specify clear expectations about the use of faculty time and effort. While the specific division of effort among teaching, research, and service would vary, every faculty member would be expected to teach undergraduates, regardless of tenure status. Even very senior, tenured faculty would be expected to teach introductory or general education courses periodically and engage with students in both structured and informal ways.

- Learning-oriented promotion and tenure criteria: Criteria for reappointment, promotion, and tenure of faculty would emphasize the quality of teaching and learning attributable to a faculty member's efforts and would use direct, authentic assessments of student learning as evidence of the degree to which any faculty member was effective in teaching. These assessments of the quality and quantity of student learning in classes would eventually replace institutional satisfaction surveys in which students rate professors on various performance criteria. New studies of students' engagement with academic work (not the National Survey of Student Engagement) would track the degree to which professors' expectations of reading, study, and writing in preparation for class were understood and applied. Faculty who sought promotion or tenure would have to demonstrate not only success in student learning, but also effectiveness in increasing students' engagement.
- Instructional role for all faculty: Faculty members in any category (tenured, tenure track, nontenure track, and contingent) would be assigned teaching responsibilities based on the learning needs of students and the qualifications of the faculty member. It would no longer be true that most introductory and general education courses were taught by contingent or non-tenure-track faculty members; students would be expected to meet and work with full-time, tenure track faculty in their first year, long before declaring a major.
- Continuous faculty development: The institution would provide strong support for faculty development in pedagogy, learning, and the assessment of learning. Regular, routine needs assessments would permit both beginning and experienced faculty members to identify professional development priorities; those priorities would be addressed through peer support, group learning, formal workshops, and individual coaching by expert colleagues. There would be no assumption that disciplinary achievement necessarily indicated teaching expertise, and there would be only support—no cultural stigma—for faculty members who sought assistance in improving their performance as teachers.
- Tighter coupling of academic and student affairs: There would be substantial evidence of collaboration between academic affairs and

student affairs. Such collaboration might take any of several forms, including the creation and assessment of learning communities with consistent faculty participation; intentional linking of classroom and experiential learning activities; integration of community service learning with course content; close and purposeful connections among all forms of advising, so that students could more coherently and effectively link academic choices with career and personal goals; and coparticipation by faculty and student affairs professional staff in first-year seminars and new student orientation.

By improving the quality and quantity of learning, colleges and universities will find that enrollment, retention, the achievement of learning outcomes, better prepared graduates, employer satisfaction, alumni loyalty, fund-raising success, and solid, evidence-based communications, marketing, and recruiting of students, faculty, and staff will all inevitably follow.

Conclusion

The sources of the primary problems in American undergraduate higher education—the lack of true higher learning, the absence of a serious culture of teaching and learning, and the consequent insufficient quality and quantity of student learning—are deeply cultural, and solving them will require fundamental, thoroughgoing changes in our colleges and universities. Taken together, these problems mean that institutions of higher education do not deliver enough value to justify their costs. Simply reducing those costs or improving the efficiency of their operations and programs would only produce institutions that fail to produce higher learning with greater efficiency.

What is needed is nonincremental change—and not just alterations in the balance sheet. Undergraduate higher education in the United States is in crisis; we are losing our minds. What we must do is clear: we must completely rethink higher education, with no exemptions or exceptions, and replace the dangerous assumptions, policies, and practices that have allowed consumer and competitive pressures to overwhelm both academic mission and common sense with strong commitments to learning as the first and most important priority. Even a superficial review of the criteria used in magazine rankings, the messages and styles used in marketing materials generated by enrollment management offices, and the priorities demonstrated in college and university budgets over the last two decades would underscore our primary concern: learning is not the touchstone for decision making in higher education. The need for change is urgent and desperate. The goal is clear: learning must become the first priority; student learning must come first. To make that possible, we, as a nation, must demand a comprehensive review of undergraduate higher education and dramatic reforms in colleges and universities of all types.

Cultural problems require cultural solutions, starting with a national conversation about what is wrong, and what is needed, in higher education. The country has the right to expect higher education to lead this conversation. For real change to occur, discussions about the quality and quantity of learning in higher education and the need for reform must occur at multiple levels, in many places, and over a significant period of time—most importantly on campuses themselves. The national conversation provides context, direction, and motive—but only many intimate and passionate conversations among colleagues in every institution of higher education can ground the discussion enough to give it enough power to bring change. Progress will not be made in improving the quality and quantity of learning—in restoring higher learning to higher education—unless both the public discussion and the multilayered, multistep processes of change on our campuses occur.

The discussions held on each campus, reinforced by the ongoing national conversation, will take every institution on its own path toward reform and renewal to improve student learning. The large-scale impact of these changes on all our campuses, in all their diversity, should be the creation of common, collective expectations and standards for higher learning that would apply broadly across higher education. If enough change occurs in enough places, and if our public expectations remain high and consistent, learning may become the touchstone for decision making; the quality and quantity of learning—documented by rigorous assessment—may become both each institution's greatest concern and the basis for comparisons between various colleges and universities; degrees may once again be earned, not delivered as entitlements; faculties may again focus on learning, rather than instruction, and on learning assessments, rather than credit hours; and every college and university might have the data and information it needs to determine and communicate the value of what it does to prospective students, parents, accrediting organizations, donors, and the public.

Most important: higher learning may return to higher education; we might no longer be losing our minds.

Notes

Chapter 1

1. Immerwahr, J., Johnson, J., Ott, A., & Rochkind, J. (2010). *Squeeze play 2010: Continued public anxiety on cost, harsher judgments on how colleges are run.* Washington, DC: The National Center for Public Policy and Higher Education & Public Agenda.
2. Association of American Colleges and Universities. (2010). *Raising the bar: Employers' views on college learning in the wake of the economic downturn.* Washington, DC: Hart Research Associates.
3. *The Futures Project: Policy for higher education in a changing world.* (1999–2005). Note: The Futures Project closed down on March 31, 2005. Information available at http://www.nerche.org/futuresproject/index.html.
4. U.S. Department of Education. (2006). *A test of leadership: Charting the future of U.S. higher education.* Washington, DC: The commission appointed by Secretary of Education Margaret Spellings.
5. Arum, R., Roksa, J., & Cho, E. (2010). *Improving undergraduate learning:* Findings and policy recommendations from the SSRC-CLA Longitudinal Project. Brooklyn, NY: Social Science Research Council.
6. Arum, R., & Roksa, J. (2010). *Academically adrift: Limited learning on college campuses* (p. 159). Chicago, IL: University of Chicago Press.
7. Blaich, C. (2007). *Overview of findings from the first year of the Wabash National Study of Liberal Education.* Retrieved from http://liberalarts.wabash.edu/research.
8. Arum, R., & Roksa, J. (2010). *Academically adrift: Limited learning on college campuses* (p. 159). Chicago, IL: University of Chicago Press.
9. Friedman, T. (2007). *The world is flat: A brief history of the twenty-first century.* New York, NY: Picador/Farrar, Straus, and Giroux.
10. Brooks, D. (2008, February 15). Fresh start conservatism. *The New York Times.* Retrieved from http://www.nytimes.com/2008/02/15/opinion/15brooks.html.
11. Damon, W. (2008). *The path to purpose: How young people find their calling in life.* New York, NY: Free Press.

12. Arnett, J. J. (2000). Emerging adulthood: A theory of development from the late teens through the twenties. *American Psychologist, 55,* 469–480.

13. Barr, R. B., & Tagg, J. (1995, November/December). From teaching to learning: A new paradigm for undergraduate education. *Change Magazine,* 13–25.

14. Bound, J., Lovenheim, M., & Turner, S. (2010). Why have college completion rates declined? An analysis of changing student preparation and collegiate resources. *American Economic Journal: Applied Economics, 2*(3), 129–157; American Institutes for Research. (2011). *Performance scorecard: Performance across 1,576 colleges.* Retrieved from http://collegemeasures .org/reporting/national/sm/default.aspx.

Chapter 2

1. See, for example, Taylor, M. C. (2010). *Crisis on campus: A bold plan for reforming our colleges and universities.* New York, NY: Alfred A. Knopf; Hacker, A., & Dreifus, C. (2010). *Higher education? How colleges are wasting our money and failing our kids—and what we can do about it.* New York, NY: Times Books, Henry Holt and Company.

2. Cheng, D., & Reed, M. (2010). *Student debt and the class of 2009.* Retrieved from The Project on Student Debt website: http://projectonstudentdebt .org/pub_view.php?idx=683.

3. U.S. Department of Education. (2006). *A test of leadership: Charting the future of U.S. higher education.* Washington, DC: The commission appointed by Secretary of Education Margaret Spellings.

4. National Center for Public Policy and Higher Education. (2008). *Measuring up 2008: The national report card on higher education.* Retrieved from http:// www.highereducation.org.

5. Jones, D. P. (2008). The information gap: Much talk, little progress. In National Center for Public Policy and Higher Education, *Measuring up 2008: the national report card on higher education.* Retrieved from http:// measuringup2008.highereducation.org/print/NCPPHEMUNationalRpt .pdf.

6. Chun, M. (2002). Looking whether the light is better: A review of the literature on assessing higher education quality. *Peer Review, 4*(2/3), 16–25.

7. National Survey of Student Engagement. (2010). *Major differences: Examining student engagement by field of study—annual results 2010.* Bloomington, IN: Indiana University Center for Postsecondary Research.

8. Middle States Commission on Higher Education. (2008). *Student learning assessment, options and resources* (2nd ed.). Retrieved from http://www .msche.org/publications/SLA_Book_0808080728085320.pdf.

9. Wolfe, T. (2004). *I am Charlotte Simmons: A novel.* New York, NY: Farrar, Straus, and Giroux.

10. Hersh, R. H., & Merrow, J. (Eds.). (2005). *Declining by degrees: Higher education at risk* (p. xi). New York, NY: Palgrave-Macmillian.
11. Seaman, B. (2005). *Binge: Campus life in an age of disconnection and excess* (p. 39). Hoboken, NJ: John Wiley & Sons.
12. Wechsler, H., & Wuethrich, B. (2002). *Dying to drink: Confronting binge drinking on college campuses.* Philadelphia, PA: Rodale Press.
13. Astin, A. W. (1996). The changing American college student: Thirty-year trends, 1966–1996. *The Review of Higher Education, 21*(2), 115–135.
14. National Survey of Student Engagement (NSSE). (2007). *Experiences that matter: Enhancing student learning and success.* Bloomington, IN: Center for Postsecondary Research, Indiana University Bloomington.
15. Brint, S., Douglass, J. A., Thomson, G., & Chatman, S. (2011). *Engaged learning in a public university: Trends in the undergraduate experience.* Report on the Results of the 2008 University of California Undergraduate Experience Survey. Center for Studies in Higher Education. University of California, Berkeley.
16. Babcock, P., & Marks, M. (2010). *Leisure College, USA: The decline in student study time.* Retrieved from the American Enterprise Institute for Public Policy Research website: http://www.aei.org/outlook/100980.
17. Botstein, L. (2005). The curriculum and college life: Confronting unfulfilled promises. In R. H. Hersh & J. Merrow (Eds.). *Declining by degrees: Higher education at risk* (pp. 209–228). New York, NY: Palgrave-Macmillian.
18. Ibid.
19. The National Center for Public Policy and Higher Education. (2004). *Measuring up 2004: The national report card on higher education.* Retrieved from http://www.highereducation.org.
20. Bok D. (2005). *Our underachieving colleges: A candid look at how much students learn and why they should be learning more.* Princeton, NJ: Princeton University Press.
21. American Association of Colleges & Universities. (2002). *Greater expectations: A new vision for learning as a nation goes to college.* Retrieved from http://www.greaterexpectations.org/pdf/GEX.FINAL.pdf.
22. American Council of Trustees and Alumni. (2009). *What will they learn? A report on general education requirements at 100 of the nation's leading colleges and universities* [Foreword]. Retrieved from https://www.goacta.org/publications/downloads/WhatWillTheyLearnFinal.pdf.
23. American Institutes for Research. (2006). *The national survey of America's college students.* Retrieved from http://www.air.org.
24. U.S. Department of Education, National Center for Education Statistics. (2007). *National Assessment of Adult Literacy: The Condition of Education.* (NCES 2007-064), Table 18-1. Retrieved from http://nces.ed.gov/pubsearch/pubsinfo.asp?pubid=2007064.

25. Pascarella, E. T., & Terenzini, P. T. (2005). *How college affects students* (Vol. 2). San Fransisco, CA: Jossey-Bass.

Chapter 3

1. Swaner, Lynn E. (2011). The theories, contexts, and multiple pedagogies of engaged learning: What succeeds and why? In D. W. Harward (Ed.), *Transforming undergraduate education: Theory that compels and practice that succeeds*. Lanham, MD: Rowman & Littlefield.
2. Freire, P. (1998). *Pedagogy of freedom: Ethics, democracy, and civic courage.* Lanham, MD: Rowman & Littlefield.
3. Swaner, Lynn E. (2008). *Degrees of complexity: A developmental view of college.* Unpublished manuscript.
4. Demarest, E. J., Reisner, E. R., Anderson, L. M., Humphrey, D. C., Farquhar, E., & Stein, S. E. (1993). *Review of research on achieving the nation's readiness goal.* Washington, DC: U.S. Department of Education.
5. Phillips, M., Brooks-Gunn, J., Duncan, G. J., Klebanov, P., & Crane, J. (1998). Family background, parenting practices, and the black-white test score gap. In C. Jencks & M. Phillips (Eds.), *The black-white test score gap* (pp. 103–148). Washington, DC: Brookings Institution Press.
6. Piaget, J. (1952). *The origins of intelligence in children.* New York, NY: International University Press; Piaget, J. (1963). *The child's conception of the world.* Paterson, NJ: Littlefield, Adams; Hersh, R. H., Paolitto, D. P., & Reimer, J. (1979). *Promoting moral growth: From Piaget to Kohlberg.* New York, NY: Longman, Inc.
7. Hersh, R. H. (1979). *Promoting moral growth: From Piaget to Kohlberg* (p. 20). New York, NY: Longman, Inc.
8. Ibid.
9. See, for example, Perry, W. G., Jr. (1970). *Forms of intellectual and ethical development in the college years: A scheme.* New York, NY: Holt, Rinehart, & Winston; Belenky, M. F., Clinchy B., Goldberger N., & Tarule, J. M. (1986). *Women's ways of knowing: The development of self, voice, and mind.* New York, NY: Basic Books; Baxter Magolda, M. B. (2004). Self-authorship as the common goal. In M. B. Baxter Magolda & P. M. King (Eds.), *Learning partnerships: Theory and models of practice to educate for self-authorship* (pp. 1–35). Sterling, VA: Stylus.
10. Chickering, A. W. (1969). *Education and identity.* San Francisco, CA: Jossey-Bass.
11. Chickering, A. W., & Reisser, L. (1993). *Education and identity* (2nd ed.). San Francisco, CA: Jossey-Bass.
12. Kadison, R., & DiGeronimo, T. F. (2004). *College of the overwhelmed: The campus mental health crisis and what to do about it.* San Francisco, CA: Jossey-Bass.

13. As described in Swaner, Lynn, E. (2005). Educating for personal and social responsibility: A review of the literature. *Liberal Education, 91*(3). 14–21.

14. Levine, A., & Cureton, J. S. (1998). *When hope and fear collide: A portrait of today's college student.* San Francisco, CA: Jossey-Bass.

15. Levine, A., and Cureton, J. S. (1998). *When hope and fear collide: A portrait of today's college student* (p. 96). San Francisco, CA: Jossey-Bass.

16. Boston College, Boston College Office of Marketing and Communications. (2007). *The journey into adulthood: Understanding student formation* [Preface]. Retrieved from http://www.bc.edu/content/dam/files/offices/mission/pdf1/umm1.pdf.

Chapter 4

1. Keeling, R. P., Dickson, J. S., & Avery, T. (2011). Neurobiology of learning. In M. London (Ed.), *Handbook of Lifelong Learning.* New York, NY and Cambridge, England: Oxford University Press.

2. Zull, J. E. (2011). *From brain to mind: Using neuroscience to guide change in education.* Sterling, VA: Stylus Publishing.

3. Neubauer, A. C., & Fink, A. (2009). Intelligence and neural efficiency. *Neuroscience & Biobehavioral Reviews, 33*(7), 1004–1023.

4. Hofstadter, D. (2007). *I am a strange loop.* New York, NY: Basic Books.

5. Chein, J., & Schneider, W. (2005). Neuroimaging studies of practice-related change: fMRI and meta-analytic evidence of a domain-general control network for learning. *Cognitive Brain Research, 25*(3), 607–623.

6. Dudai, Y. (1989). *Neurobiology of memory: Concepts, findings, trends.* Oxford, England: Oxford University Press; Raichle, M. E., & Mintun, M. A. (2006). Brain work and brain imaging. *Annual Review of Neuroscience, 29,* 449–76.

7. Welberg, L. (2009). Neuroimaging: Learning changes the resting brain. *Nature Reviews Neuroscience, 10*(11), 766–767.

8. Spierer, L., Tardif, E., Sperdin, H., Murray, M. M., & Clarke, S. (2007). Learning-induced plasticity in auditory spatial representations revealed by electrical neuroimaging. *The Journal of Neuroscience, 27*(20), 5474–5483.

9. Dehaene, S., Pegado, F., Braga, L. W., Ventura, P., Filho, G. N., Jobert, A., Dehaene-Lambertz, G., et al. (2010). How learning to read changes the cortical networks for vision and language. *Science, 330*(6009), 1359–1364.

10. Vytal, K. (2010). Neuroimaging support for discrete neural correlates of basic emotions: A voxel-based meta-analysis. *Journal of Cognitive Neuroscience, 22*(12), 2864–2885.

11. Ashby, F. G., & Maddox, W. T. (2005). Human category learning. *Annual Review of Psychology, 56*(1), 149–178; Rawley, J. B., & Constantinidis, C. (2009). Neural correlates of learning and working memory in the primate posterior parietal cortex. *Neurobiology of Learning and Memory, 91*(2),

129–138; Rumbaugh, D. M., King, J. E., Beran, M. J., Washburn, D. A., & Gould, K. L. (2007). A salience theory of learning and behavior—with perspectives on neurobiology and cognition. *International Journal of Primatology, 28,* 973–996.

12. Grigorenko, E. L., & Naples, A. J. (2008). *Single-word reading: behavioral and biological perspectives.* New York, NY: Lawrence Erlbaum Associates.

13. Begley, S. (2008). *Train your mind, change your brain: How a new science reveals our extraordinary potential to transform ourselves.* New York, NY: Balantine Books.; Jensen, E. (2000). Brain-based learning—A reality check. *Educational Leadership, 57*(7), 76–79.

14. Mareschal, D., Johnson, M. H., Sirois, S., Spratling, M., Thomas, M., & Westermann, G. (2007). *Neuroconstructivism: How the brain constructs cognition* (Vol. 1). Oxford, England: Oxford University Press.

15. Dewey, J. (1938). *Experience and education.* West Lafayette, IN: Kappa Delta Pi; Piaget, J. (1972). Intellectual evolution from adolescence to adulthood. *Vita Humana, 15,* 1–12.

16. Malberg, J., Eisch, A., & Nestler, E. (2000). Chronic antidepressant treatment increases neurogenesis in adult rat hippocampus. *The Journal of Neuroscience, 20*(24), 9104–9110.

17. Cranford, J., Eisenberg, D., & Serras, A. (2009). Substance use behaviors, mental health problems, and use of mental health services in a probability sample of college students. *Addictive Behaviors, 34*(2), 134–145; Garlow, S. J., Rosenberg, J., Moore, J. D., Haas, A. P., Koestner, B., Hendin, H., & Nemeroff, C. B. (2008). Depression, desperation, and suicidal ideation in college students: Results from the American Foundation for Suicide Prevention College Screening Project at Emory University. *Depression and Anxiety, 25*(6).

18. Harvey. P. O., Fossati, P., Pochon, J. B., Levy, R., Lebastard, G., et al. (2005). Cognitive control and brain resources in major depression: An MRI study using the n-back task. *Neuroimage, 26*(3), 860–869.

19. Doidge, Norman (2007). *The brain that changes itself: Stories of personal triumph from the frontiers of brain science.* New York, NY: Penguin Group; Cicchetti, D., & Curtis, W. J. (2006). The developing brain and neural plasticity: Implications for normality, psychopathology, and resilience. In D. Cicchetti & D. J. Cohen (Eds.), *Developmental psychopathology: Developmental neuroscience* (2nd ed., p. 11), New York, NY: Wiley Publishing; Eriksson, P. (1998). Neurogenesis in the adult human hippocampus. *Nature Medicine, 4,* 1313–1317.

20. Willis, J. (2008). Building a bridge from neuroscience to the classroom. *Phi Delta Kappan, 89*(6), 424–427.

21. Gogtay, N. (2004). Dynamic mapping of human cortical development during childhood through early adulthood. *Proceedings of the National Academy of Sciences, 101,* 8174–8179; Seeman, P. (1999) Images in neuroscience:

Brain development, X: Pruning during development. *American Journal of Psychiatry, 156,* 168.

22. Kottlow, M., Praeg, E., & Luethy, C. (2010). Artists' advance: Decreased upper alpha power while drawing in artists compared with non-artists. *Brain Topography, 23,* 392–402.

23. Samuels, S. J. (2004). Toward a theory of automatic information processing in reading, revisited. In R. B. Ruddell & N. J. Unrau (Eds.), *Theoretical models and processes of reading* (5th ed., pp. 1127-1148). Newark, DE: International Reading Association.

24. Mancia, M. (1983). Archaeology of Freudian thought and the history of neurophysiology. *International Review of Psychoanalysis, 10,* 185–192.

25. Tokuhama-Espinosa, T. (2010). *Mind, brain, and education science: A comprehensive guide to the new brain-based teaching.* New York, NY: W. W. Norton & Company.

Chapter 5

1. National Research Council. (2000). *How people learn: Brain, mind, experience, and school.* Washington, DC: National Academy Press.

2. Ewell, P. T., National Institute for Learning Outcomes Assessment. (2009). *Assessment, accountability, and improvement: Revisiting the tension.* Champaign, IL: University of Illinois at Urbana-Champaign.

3. Kuh, G. D. (2007). Risky business: Promises and pitfalls of institutional transparency. *Change, 39*(5), 30–35; Miller, M. A., & Ewell, P. T. (2005). *Measuring up on college-level learning.* San Jose, CA: National Center for Public Policy and Higher Education.

4. The National Center for Public Policy and Higher Education. (2008). *Measuring up 2008: The national report card on higher education.* San Jose, CA: Author.

5. Merisotis J. P., Lumina Foundation for Education. (2009, October 14). The Howard R. Bowen Lecture, Claremont Graduate University, Claremont, CA.

6. Gawande, A. (2004, December 6). The bell curve. *The New Yorker.*

7. Ibid.

8. Banta, T. W., Griffin, M., Flateby, T. L., & Kahn, S. (2009). Three promising alternatives for assessing college students' knowledge and skills (NILOA Occasional Paper No. 2). Urbana, IL: University of Illinois and Indiana University, National Institute of Learning Outcomes Assessment.

9. Pirsig, R. M. (1974). *Zen and the art of motorcycle maintenance: An inquiry into values.* New York, NY: William Morrow.

10. *Collegiate Learning Assessment: Common Scoring Criteria* (2008). Retrieved from http://www.cae.org/content/pdf/CLA_Scoring_Criteria_(Jan%202008).pdf. Reproduced with permission of the Council for Aid to Education.

11. For an elaborated response to these questions accompanied by qualitative criteria, see the appendix in Hardison, C., Hong, E.,Chun, M., Kugelmass, H., & Nemeth, A. (2009). *Architecture of the CLA Tasks*. Retrieved from http://www.collegiatelearningassessment.org/files/Architecture of the CLA Tasks.pdf.

12. *VALUE: Valid assessment of learning in undergraduate education project: A project of the American Association of Colleges and Universities*. (May 2007–April 2010). Retrieved from http://www.aacu.org/value.

13. Banta, T. W., Jones, E. A., & Black, K. E. (2009). Planning, implementing, and improving assessment in higher education. In *Designing effective assessment: Principles and profiles of good practice* (p. 6). New York, NY: Jossey-Bass.

14. Wenger, E. M. (1998). *Communities of practice: Learning, meaning, and identity*. New York, NY: Cambridge University Press.

15. Wenger, E. (2006). *Communities of practice: A brief introduction*. Retrieved from http://www.ewenger.com/theory.

16. Metcalfe, J., & Kornell, N. *Principles of cognitive science in education: The effects of generation, errors, and feedback*. Retrieved from http://pbr.psycho nomic-journals.org/content/14/2/225.full.pdf; Roediger, H. L., III, McDaniel, M., & McDermott, K. *Test enhanced learning*. Retrieved from http://www.psychologicalscience.org/observer/getArticle.cfm?id=1951.

17. Wiggins, G. (1990). The case for authentic assessment. *Practical Assessment, Research & Evaluation, 2*(2).

Chapter 6

1. See, for example, Alexander, L. (2009, October 17). The three year solution: How the reinvention of higher education benefits parents, students, and schools. *Newsweek*. Retrieved from http://www.newsweek.com/2009/10/16/the-three-year-solution.html.

2. The Association of American Colleges and Universities (AAC&U). (2010). See statement by President Carol Geary Schneider, Ph.D. The three year degree is no silver bullet. In it President Schneider writes, "For the overwhelming majority of American college students, a mere three years of college study might leave them with a piece of paper, but not with a degree that has real value; it would foreclose their opportunity for a truly empowering education. And our nation, too, would be left without the well-educated citizens needed to rebuild our economy and strengthen our democratic values and traditions for our shared future security and prosperity." Retrieved from http://www.aacu.org/about/statements/2010/threeyears.cfm.

3. Jaeger A. J., & Eagan, M. K. (2010). Examining retention and contingent faculty use in a state system of public higher education. *Educational Policy, 24*(4), 1–31.

4. Taber, C. S., & Lodge, M. (2006). Motivated skepticism in the evaluation of political beliefs. *American Journal of Political Science, 50*(3), 755–769; Westen, D., Blagov, P. S., Harenski, K., Kilts, C., and Hamann, S. (2006). Neural bases of motivated reasoning: An fMRI study of emotional constraints on partisan political judgment in the 2004 U.S. presidential election. *Journal of Cognitive Neuroscience, 18*(11): 1947–1958.

5. Williams, M. M. (2005, March 31). Look back: Coping with a new menace: The computer. *Discover Magazine Online.* Retrieved from http://discover magazine.com/2005/mar/look-back-computer.

6. Hersh, R. H. (1983). How to avoid becoming a nation of technopeasants. *Phi Delta Kappan, 64*(9), 635–638.

7. Stross, R. (2010, July 9). Computers at home: Educational hope vs. teenage reality. *The New York Times.* Retrieved from http://www.nytimes .com/2010/07/11/business/11digi.html?_r=1&emc=eta1.

8. See, for example, Carr, N. (2010). *The shallows: What the Internet is doing to our brains.* New York, NY: Norton.

9. Prewitt, K. (1983, November/December). Civic education and scientific illiteracy. *Journal of Teacher Education,* 17–20.

10. Smith, M. K. (2005). Eliot W. Eisner, connoisseurship, criticism and the art of education. *The Encyclopedia of Informal Education* (p. 4). Retrieved from www.infed.org/thinkers/eisner.htm.

11. Prewitt, K. (1983, November/December). Civic education and scientific illiteracy. *Journal of Teacher Education,* 17.

12. Friedman, T. L. (2005). *The world is flat: A brief history of the twenty-first century.* New York, NY: Farrar, Straus, and Giroux.

13. Prewitt, K. (1983, November/December). Civic education and scientific illiteracy. *Journal of Teacher Education,* 17–20.

14. Eisner, E. (1998). *The enlightened eye: Qualitative inquiry and the enhancement of educational practice (p. 63).* Upper Saddle River, NJ: Merrill.

15. Moon, Y. (2010). *Different* (p. 2). New York, NY: Crown Business.

16. Moon, Y. (2010). *Different* (p. 5). New York, NY: Crown Business.

17. Schneider, B. L., & Kessler, V. S. (2007). School reform 2007: Transforming education into a scientific enterprise. *Annual Review of Sociology, 33,* 197–217; Noble, K., Casey, B., & Tottenham, N. (2005). Neuroscience perspectives on disparities in school readiness and cognitive achievement. *The Future of Children, 15*(1), 71–89.

18. Evans, M. D. R., et. al. (2010). Family scholarly and educational success: Books and schooling in 27 nations. *Research in Social Stratification and Mobility, 28,* 171–197.

19. Evans, M.D.R., et. al. (2010). Family scholarly and educational success: Books and schooling in 27 nations. *Research in Social Stratification and Mobility, 28,* 187.

20. Barr, R. B., & Tagg, J. (1995, November/December). From teaching to learning: A new paradigm for undergraduate education. *Change Magazine*, 13–25.
21. Arum, R., & Roksa, J. (2010). *Academically adrift: Limited learning on college campuses*. Chicago, IL: University of Chicago Press.
22. Wilson, R. (2010, July 9). Tenure, RIP: What the vanishing status means for the future of education. *Chronicle of Higher Education*. Retrieved from http://chronicle.com/article/Tenure-RIP/66114.
23. For an interesting perspective on these questions that shows how old discussion of these issues is, see Education: The Great Conversation, a review of Robert Maynard Hutchins' *The Conflict in Education*. In Time (1953, September 21). Retrieved from http://www.time.com/time/magazine/article/0,9171,890674,00.html.
24. Whitehead, A. N. (1929). *Aims of education (p. 4)*. New York, NY: The Free Press.
25. For an excellent explication of the value and use of learning portfolios, see Zubizuretta, J. (2004). *The learning portfolio: Reflective practice for improving student learning*. San Francisco, CA: Anker Press/Jossey-Bass.

Index

AAC&U. *See* Association of American Colleges and Universities

Academically Adrift: Limited Learning on College Campuses (Arum and Roksa), 10

academic expectations, elevated
challenging and rigorous curriculum, need for, 134
future plan for, 3, 172
vs. what is available, 9–10

academic expectations, low
as accepted norm in campus life, 35–36
alcohol abuse and, 35
change in, need for, 152–55
consumer preferences and social activities, focus on, 13–14, 36–37
in elite institutions, 36–37
from faculty, 14–15, 20, 35–37
from students, 2, 4–6, 8–9, 14, 134
teaching and learning, lack of focus on, 14–15, 20

academic freedom, assessments and, 34

academic learning, defined, 11, 42, 64

academic performance
decline in, 37–38, 164
high-risk drinking and, 35
student performance, evaluating, 30–31

accommodation, process of, 48–51

accountability, institutional
arguments against, 86–87
demand for, 83–86
faculty/institutional resistance to, 9–10, 28, 33–34, 83, 85, 106
lack of, 9–10, 15, 28–29
learning-based accountability, 86–87
No Child Left Behind (NCLB) and, 84, 87
quantitative vs. qualitative focus of, 16–17
state-by-state comparisons, 28–29
See also assessments, learning

accountability, lack of
for teachers, 2, 18–21, 44
for undergraduates, 2, 18–21
See also accountability, institutional

ACT/SAT scores
as assessment tool, 129
as job success indicator, 31
as state-by-state comparative data, 29

addiction, 61, 79
See also alcohol/alcohol abuse; behavioral issues

adjunct faculty, use of, 14–15, 134–36, 156–57

administrative bloat, 14, 149–51

advising/mentoring, importance of, 48, 136–37, 140–41, 172

AIR. *See* Association for Institutional Research